Antonette Kuzmanich Hafen

Food for Fellowship
COOKBOOK

Other books by Antoinette Kuzmanich Hatfield

ReMARKable Recipes
More ReMARKable Recipes

Food for Fellowship
COOKBOOK

from the recipe files of Mrs. Mark O. Hatfield

by

ANTOINETTE KUZMANICH HATFIELD

WORD BOOKS, PUBLISHER
Waco, Texas

To Grandad and Dida

Mrs. Hatfield prepares piquant sauce for Rock Cornish game hens (recipe, page 80)

FOOD FOR FELLOWSHIP

INTRODUCTION

Fellowship in the early Church meant getting together for the purpose of sharing and sustaining each other in their belief in Jesus Christ. Today we seem to have become so formalized in our worship that sometimes we wonder if the fellowship which sustained the early Church has been lost. Are we really helping one another to grow spiritually as individuals and as a body of believers? One ingredient that cannot be provided except through Christ is His unique love for all mankind.

It is hoped that this book will help you as you plan Christ-centered meals—*Food for Fellowship*—meals you and like-minded persons can gather to share as you uphold your common belief in salvation through Christ. Christ often used mealtime to teach—the Wedding Feast at Cana, the Sermon on the Mount, the Last Supper.

In the early Church the members needed to have nourishment not only for the body, but, more importantly, for the spirit. They needed to encourage each other in their beliefs, in their life-styles, and in their witness before others who might desire to join them as a band of believers.

Over the years this "band" has grown, but the idea of sustaining each other seems to have diminished. Is it not time once again to renew our commitment to our Lord and Savior Jesus Christ, and to provide Food for Fellowship for others who now believe or who would believe?

ANTOINETTE KUZMANICH HATFIELD

Bethesda, Maryland
March, 1972

What we have seen and heard we declare to you,
so that you and we together may share in a common life,
that life which we share with the Father and his Son Jesus Christ.
1 John 1:3, NEB

SUNDAY SCHOOL BREAKFAST

Jesus said, "Come and have breakfast." None of the disciples dared to ask, "Who are you?" They knew it was the Lord. Jesus now came up, took the bread, and gave it to them, and the fish in the same way (John 21:12–14, NEB).

Traditionally you may think of having a Sunday School Breakfast only after an Easter Sunrise Service. In limiting this "feast" to such an occasional gathering, you can miss much of the fellowship in "breaking bread together" prior to the study of God's Word. Fellowship around the breakfast table will often set the scene in a receptive atmosphere for an in-depth sharing and discussing of your faith. Why not try to have a Sunday School Breakfast at least once a month?

Make citrus cups by cutting oranges in half, scooping out the slices with a grapefruit knife and then making saw-toothed edges. First cut slashes all one direction in orange shell; then cut the other direction. Fill shells with chilled fresh fruit and garnish with mint leaves.

Citrus Fruit Cups
Sausage
*B. J.'s Pancakes with
*Grandmother's Homemade Syrup
Milk   Coffee   Tea

Melon Rings Filled with Berries
Bacon and Scrambled Eggs
*"No-Beat" Popovers with
*Orange Butter
or *Heritage Coffee Cake
Milk   Coffee   Tea

B. J.'S PANCAKES
About 30 5-inch pancakes

1 cup flour, plus 2 tablespoons
2 teaspoons soda
2½ teaspoons baking powder
1 teaspoon salt
1 cup quick-cooking rolled oats

1 cup bran cereal
2 tablespoons brown sugar
2 eggs, slightly beaten
3 tablespoons salad oil
3 cups buttermilk

Sift flour and measure; sift with soda, baking powder, and salt. In a large bowl combine oats, bran, brown sugar, and flour mixture and mix together. Add eggs, oil, and buttermilk. • Mix quickly. Don't overbeat. Give just enough quick strokes to moisten the dry ingredients. Ignore the lumps. • Before cooking, test the griddle by sprinkling a few drops of cold water on it. If the water bounces and sputters, the griddle is ready to use. Cook pancakes on lightly greased griddle over medium heat. Turn when bubbles appear.

Never cease to love your fellow-Christians. Remember to show hospitality. There are some who, by so doing, have entertained angels without knowing it (Hebrews 13:1).

GRANDMOTHER'S HOMEMADE SYRUP
About 2 cups

1½ cups white sugar
½ cup brown sugar
1 cup water

¾ teaspoon maple flavoring
½ teaspoon vanilla extract
(use more or less to suit taste)

Combine sugar and water. Boil until sugar is dissolved. Just before serving, add maple flavoring and vanilla.

To keep pancakes warm, place them on a toweled baking sheet—well separated by a tea towel—in a 200 degree oven. Or fold a sort of cloth file in which to store them. Never stack pancakes in oven without cloth, for the steam they produce will make them flabby.

Grandmother's homemade syrup will stay warm for a longer time if poured into a small silver pitcher.

14

After breakfast, Jesus said to Simon Peter, "Simon son of John, do you love me more than all else?" "Yes, Lord," he answered, "you know I love you." "Then tend my sheep" (John 21:15, NEB).

"NO-BEAT" POPOVERS   *12 popovers*

2 eggs   1 cup flour
1 cup milk   ½ teaspoon salt
1 tablespoon melted butter

Grease popover pans and set aside. • Break eggs into bowl. Add milk, butter, flour, and salt. Mix well with spoon, disregarding lumps. • Fill pans ¾ full. Place in cold oven. Set control at 450 degrees and turn on heat. • Bake for 30 minutes. (The secret is starting with a cold oven.) Do not peek for 30 minutes. Serve immediately.

Popovers need bottom heat only. Set your oven so that the upper heating element does not come on. Have all ingredients about 75 degrees before mixing.

or

Preheat oven to 450 degrees. Place glass or earthenware cups on baking sheet to heat. • Measure all ingredients into bowl and beat with rotary beater until mixture is smooth. • Remove cups from oven and grease each with ⅓ teaspoon butter. Fill cups with batter until half full. Bake at once. • After 15 minutes lower the heat to 350 degrees, without peeping. Bake 20 minutes longer. • To test for doneness, remove a popover to be sure the side walls are firm. If they are not cooked long enough, the popovers will collapse. Insert a sharp knife into the other popovers to let steam escape, after baking.

NOTE: Do not attempt to double this recipe. Make separate batches.

15

ORANGE BUTTER *1 pound*

4 oranges, juice from all
   4, peel from only 2

½ pound confectioners' sugar
1 pound (4 sticks) butter

Grate the orange part of the peel from only 2 of the oranges. Extract the juice from all 4 and strain. Add the peel to the juice; then combine the sugar with it and dissolve the sugar in the juice as much as possible. • Soften the butter in an electric mixer. Add the juice mixture and beat until well blended. • Mold butter or place in jelly jar and chill in the refrigerator before serving. This butter is also marvelous with dinner rolls, breakfast toast, pancakes, or waffles as well as popovers.

HERITAGE COFFEE CAKE *16 servings*

1 cup (2 sticks) butter
2 cups sugar
6 eggs, separated plus 1
   egg white
1½ cups flour
½ teaspoon salt

2 teaspoons baking powder
6 tablespoons milk
1 teaspoon vanilla extract
½ teaspoon almond extract
confectioners' sugar

Cream butter until light. Add sugar slowly while continuing to beat until light and fluffy. Beat in egg yolks, one at a time. • Sift dry ingredients together and add alternately with milk which has been mixed with the vanilla and almond flavorings. Beat egg whites until stiff; then fold gently into batter. • Pour into well-greased Bundt cake pan. • Bake at 350 degrees for 1 hour or until cake tests done. Invert on cake rack to cool. Remove from pan. Sift confectioners' sugar over the top.

PRESCHOOLER
SUNDAY SCHOOL SNACKS

Jesus said to them, "Let the children come to me; do not try to stop them; for the kingdom of Heaven belongs to such as these" (Matthew 19:14, NEB).

Sunday school can be made a very special time for young children. While they are learning the Word of God, many children often need a snack. Because their energy and attention span is somewhat limited, a stop to refuel with one of the included recipes or suggestions could be made. All parents should be asked if their children may be served. This is soon established with regular attenders, but do not forget to ask parents of visitors or new members when they arrive with their children.

Cheese and Crackers
Fresh Fruit Slices
Graham Crackers and Juice
*Old-fashioned German Sugar Cookies
*Gingerbread

Serve fruit when the children are studying seeds. Let them watch you cut the fruit open; give them the opportunity to find and examine the seeds. Then slice the fruit and serve it. Apples, bananas, and pears are good fruits to use.

Train up a child in the way he should go, and when he is old he will not depart from it (Proverbs 22:6, RSV).

OLD-FASHIONED GERMAN SUGAR COOKIES
6 dozen

Decorate the German cookies for special occasions.

2 cups margarine or butter
2 cups sugar
4 eggs
1 teaspoon soda

1 teaspoon salt
5 cups flour (approx.)
flavoring—lemon, almond, and vanilla extract

Cream together the butter and sugar. Then add eggs, one at a time, and beat until creamy. Dissolve soda and salt in buttermilk and add to butter mixture alternately with flour to make a soft dough. • Divide into thirds and add a different flavoring to each batch. Chill. Roll out on heavy pastry board sprinkled with sugar; cut with different shaped cookie cutters. • Bake in preheated 350 degree oven for 10 to 12 minutes. Cool. Store in tight containers. These may be frozen.

GINGERBREAD   *24 servings*

Little muffins made from a yellow cake mix and glazed with a thin powdered sugar icing are popular with the preschool crowd and very easy to make.

1 cup shortening
1¼ cups granulated sugar
3 eggs
1¼ cups dark molasses
4 cups sifted flour
1¼ tablespoons baking powder

1 teaspoon ginger
1 teaspoon allspice
1 teaspoon cinnamon
½ teaspoon cloves
2 teaspoons salt
1¾ cups boiling water

Preheat oven to 325 degrees. Grease a 12 x 17-inch pan or petite muffin pans. • Cream shortening and sugar. Add eggs and molasses and beat. Sift dry ingredients together. Add dry ingredients alternately with boiling water to butter mixture. Continue beating until blended. • Pour into prepared pan. Bake for about 25 minutes.

BRUNCH
FOLLOWING FIRST SERVICE

Be hospitable to one another without complaining. Whatever gift each of you may have received, use it in service to one another, like good stewards dispensing the grace of God in its varied forms (1 Peter 4:9–10, NEB).

Have you ever thought of asking your neighbors to hear a particular sermon and then to come over to eat afterwards? Your dining table is a place of fellowship where you can naturally share what Christ means to you. Why not share your gift of hospitality with your neighbors?

*Bacon Quiche or *Soup Senegalese
*Saucy Meatballs à la Edi Mae
Fruit Platter or *Chafing Dish Tomatoes
*Evelyn's Oatmeal Cookies
Coffee   Tea

Contribute to the needs of God's people, and practise hospitality (Romans 12:13, NEB).

A beautifully arranged fruit platter may serve as the centerpiece for a buffet as well as make a delicious salad. For color, use strawberries, watermelon balls, or maraschino cherries with canned and seasonal fruits. The platter may be arranged ahead of time, covered with plastic wrap, and refrigerated, if the fruits that discolor are covered with lemon juice or acid dressing. Dip banana slices in lemon juice and sprinkle with angel flake coconut.

BACON QUICHE   *6 servings*

Quiche is always served lukewarm. It may be baked ahead and frozen. Reheat by placing it, un-thawed, in a 350 degree oven for 30 to 50 minutes. Quiche may be served as an appetizer baked in tiny tartlet pans. Cut down cooking time for tartlets.

1 9-inch unbaked pastry shell
1 pound bacon
3 eggs, beaten
¾ cup evaporated milk
½ teaspoon salt

¼ teaspoon nutmeg
½ teaspoon Worcestershire sauce
1 cup shredded Swiss cheese
1 3½-ounce can French fried onions

Fry bacon until crisp; drain. Reserve 6 to 8 slices crisp bacon for garnish. Crumble balance. • Combine eggs, milk, salt, nut-meg, and Worcestershire sauce. Stir in cheese. Sprinkle onions and crumbled bacon over unbaked shell. Pour egg mixture over all. • Bake at 325 degrees until golden brown for 25 to 30 min-utes. Serve warm, cut into wedges. Garnish with crisp bacon slices.

I give you a new commandment: love one another; as I have loved you, so you are to love one another. If there is this love among you, then all will know that you are my disciples (John 13:34–35, NEB).

SOUP SENEGALESE   *12 servings*

4 leeks, white part
1 medium onion
1 stalk celery
¼ cup (½ stick) sweet butter
5 medium potatoes
1 quart chicken broth

1 tablespoon salt
3 cups half and half cream
1 teaspoon curry powder
pepper to taste
1 cup heavy cream

Finely slice the white part of the leeks, the onion, and the celery. Brown very lightly in sweet butter. Add potatoes which have been finely sliced. Stir in chicken broth and salt; boil for 40 minutes. • Force cooked mixture through a fine strainer. Return to heat and add half and half cream. Season to taste with curry powder, salt, and pepper and bring to boil. • Cool and then rub through a fine strainer again. When the soup is cold, add heavy cream. • Chill thoroughly before serving. Garnish with finely chopped apple and finely chopped breast of chicken.

SAUCY MEATBALLS À LA EDI MAE
50 meatballs

1 pound ground round steak
2 tablespoons bread crumbs
1 egg, slightly beaten
¾ teaspoon salt
dash black pepper
⅓ cup onion, finely chopped
⅓ cup green pepper, finely
  chopped

2 tablespoons butter
1 can tomato soup
2 tablespoons brown sugar
1 tablespoon Worcestershire
  sauce
1 teaspoon steak sauce
1 tablespoon prepared mustard
1 tablespoon vinegar

Mix beef, crumbs, egg, salt, and black pepper. Shape into 50 balls. Place in shallow 13 x 9 x 2-inch baking pan. Broil until brown; turn once (don't overbrown). Remove meatballs to 3-quart casserole which has cover. • In saucepan, sauté onion and green pepper in butter until tender. Stir in remaining ingredients. Pour sauce over meatballs. • Cover and bake at 350 degrees for 20 minutes. This recipe can be doubled and also can be frozen.

Reheat thawed meatballs in chafing dish or electric skillet. I made over 600 of these for a wedding reception for the children's Sunday school teacher when her daughter was married.

CHAFING DISH TOMATOES   *16 servings*

½ cup (1 stick) butter

1 tablespoon sweet basil

½ cup fresh chopped parsley

4 baskets cherry tomatoes

In chafing dish melt butter and add sweet basil. Then add tomatoes and heat. Sprinkle with chopped parsley. Serve with spoon.

Do you give service? Give it as in the strength which God supplies (1 Peter 4:11, NEB).

EVELYN'S OATMEAL COOKIES
1½ to 2 dozen

1 cup shortening

1 cup granulated sugar

½ cup brown sugar

1 egg, beaten

1½ cups flour

1 teaspoon soda

1 teaspoon cinnamon

1½ cups quick rolled oats

¾ cup finely chopped nuts

1 teaspoon vanilla extract

Cream shortening, granulated sugar, and brown sugar. Add beaten egg. Sift together the flour, soda, and cinnamon; add it to the first mixture and stir. Add and mix in oats, finely chopped nuts, and vanilla. • Chill for 1 hour. Form into walnut-sized balls. Place on greased cookie sheet 2 inches apart. • Butter bottom of glass and dip it in granulated sugar; flatten out the cookies with the glass. Redip the glass in sugar each time. • Bake for 8 to 10 minutes at 350 degrees. Makes 18 large or 24 medium cookies.

COFFEE HOUR

In all our prayers to God, the Father of our Lord Jesus Christ, we thank him for you, because we have heard of the faith you hold in Christ Jesus, and the love you bear towards all God's people (Colossians 1:3, NEB).

The Coffee Hour at the church after the worship service is just one way to make the visitor to your church feel welcome. The red rose or the colored ribbon may be used as a mark of identification, but hospitality after church may be the one ingredient that keeps the newcomer coming back. Make an effort to get acquainted with the visitor and better acquainted with the members of your church. The Coffee Hour may be as simple or elaborate as you like. Hot coffee and hospitality are the only essentials.

The most important thing in coffee making is the cleanliness of the pot. It should be scrubbed well after each use; it may be rinsed with water in which a few teaspoons of baking soda have been dissolved and then scalded. You might remember that the taste of the water affects the flavor of the coffee—the purer the water the better the result.

Cranberry Juice

Coffee   Tea

* Mayor Beck's Danish Butter Balls

* Spicy Donut Balls

* Italian Cookies

* Banana Nut Bread

MAYOR BECK'S DANISH BUTTER BALLS
3 dozen

1 cup butter
½ cup powdered sugar
1 cup pecans, finely chopped

1 teaspoon vanilla
2 cups flour

Cream together the butter and powdered sugar. Add other ingredients. Work with hands. Make into 1-inch balls. Put on greased cookie sheet. Bake ½ hour at 300 degrees. Cool and roll in powdered sugar.

For judging the temperature of the cooking oil, use a deep-fat thermometer. Nothing is more important in frying than proper temperatures. One wise old gourmet said, "The food must be surprised by the hot fat."

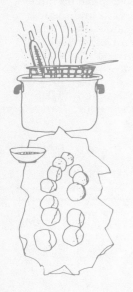

SPICY DONUT BALLS   *About 45*

3¼ cups sifted flour
2 teaspoons baking powder
½ teaspoon cinnamon
¼ teaspoon nutmeg
¼ teaspoon allspice
dash of salt
2 eggs

⅔ cup sugar
1 teaspoon vanilla extract
⅔ cup light cream
½ cup (1 stick) butter or
    margarine, melted
½ cup sugar
½ teaspoon cinnamon

Sift together flour, baking powder, spices, and dash of salt. Beat together eggs, sugar, and vanilla until thick and lemon colored. Combine cream and butter or margarine. • Alternately add dry ingredients and cream mixture, half at a time, to egg mixture. Beat just until blended after each addition. • Chill dough 2 hours. Roll ⅜-inch thick on floured surface; cut dough with 1-inch cutter and roll into balls. • Fry in deep hot fat at 375 degress, turning once. Allow about 1 minute on each side. Drain on paper toweling; while warm, shake donuts in a mixture of ½ cup sugar and ½ teaspoon cinnamon.

I wish you could understand how deep is my anxiety for you, and for those at Laodicea, and for all who have never met me. How I long that you may be encouraged, and find out more and more how strong are the bonds of Christian love (Colossians 2:1–2, Phillips).

ITALIAN COOKIES

4 eggs
1½ cups sugar
½ cup butter, melted
½ cup shortening, melted
1 cup evaporated milk
2 tablespoons anise extract
1 tablespoon anise seeds

3 cups flour
1 teaspoon baking soda
1 teaspoon baking powder
½ teaspoon salt
1 cup almonds, blanched,
    coarsely chopped

Beat the eggs and sugar well. Add the melted butter and shortening, milk, anise, anise seeds to egg mixture. • Sift flour before measuring; then sift together with soda, baking powder, and salt and add to the mixture. Add almonds. (It gets hard to mix after almonds are added.) • Roll to finger thickness. (Be sure board is well floured when rolling.) • Bake in one piece on greased cookie sheet at 350 degrees for 10 minutes. • When

Freeze one large or two small loaves of banana bread. Slice horizontally into 3 equal layers and fill layers with cream cheese filling. Beat one 8-ounce package cream cheese until fluffy. Divide into 2 bowls. In one bowl add ¼ cup finely chopped maraschino cherries; beat until pink; then add another ¼ cup quartered cherries. In other bowl add ¼ cup finely chopped dried apricots to cheese, beat, and add ¼ cup more. After filling and putting together layers, wrap loaves in foil and freeze. When removed from freezer, frost loaves with 8-ounce cream cheese beaten until fluffy.

baked, cut into 1½ x ½-inch sticks while still warm. Place on baking sheet, put into 350 degree oven, and toast for 3 to 5 minutes. These are hard cookies. They keep well.

Next, as regards brotherly love, you don't need any written instructions. God himself is teaching you to love one another and you are already extending your love to all the Macedonians. Yet we urge you to have more and more of this love, and to make it your ambition to have no ambition! Be busy with your own affairs and do your work yourselves. The result will be a reputation for honesty in the world outside and an honorable independence (1 Thessalonians 4:9–12, Phillips).

BANANA NUT BREAD   *4 small loaves*

¾ cup shortening	¾ teaspoon soda
1½ cups sugar	1 teaspoon salt
3 eggs, beaten	4½ teaspoons milk
1½ cups ripe banana pulp	1½ teaspoons lemon juice
3 cups flour	1½ cups nuts, coarsely
2¼ teaspoons baking powder	chopped

Preheat oven to 350 degrees. Grease 4 small or 2 regular size loaf pans. • Cream shortening and sugar. Beat in beaten eggs and bananas. Sift together flour, baking powder, soda, and salt. Add the sifted ingredients in about 3 parts to the mixture. Beat the batter after each addition until smooth. Add milk and lemon juice and mix well. Fold in chopped nuts. Pour into prepared pans. Bake for about 55 minutes.

DINNER
FOLLOWING 11:00 SERVICE

See, I stand knocking at the door. If anyone listens to my voice and opens the door, I will go into his house and dine with him, and he with me (Revelation 3:20, Phillips).

In the early Church we read of many examples of the Christians gathering to "break bread," to exchange views, and to pray for and with each other. How long has it been since you prayed with someone outside of a church building? How long has it been since you've told someone the good news . . . the story of salvation . . . or what your faith is? How long has it been since you've been a servant of the Lord . . . worked His fields . . . sowed His seeds . . . and waited for the harvest? Even a special meal for your own family will make Sunday the Lord's Day and Family Day—a special time for your children to remember.

Marian's Cold Gazpacho Soup

Marian's Pot Roast

Potato Soufflé

Vegetable Salad

Rolls   Coffee

Lemon Ribbon-Layered Meringue Pie

At a dinner after church, parents and the younger set should all be able to relax. As a welcoming note, serve the cold gazpacho in cups, colorful mugs, or parfait glasses in the living room while you finish up the rest of the dinner.

27

MARIAN'S COLD GAZPACHO SOUP   *12 cups*

1 medium green pepper,
  chopped fine
1 medium onion, chopped fine
2 medium tomatoes, peeled
  and chopped fine
2 1-quart, 14-ounce cans
  tomato juice
1½ teaspoons hot pepper sauce
1 clove garlic, minced

3 tablespoons white vinegar
⅓ cup olive oil
1 tablespoon plus 1 teaspoon
  Worcestershire sauce
salt and pepper to taste
2 cucumbers, thinly sliced for
  garnish
2 tomatoes, chopped for
  garnish

Place the chopped pepper, onion, and tomatoes in a bowl and then add all remaining ingredients except garnishes. Season with salt and pepper to taste. • Mix well and chill well. Serve individual portions topped with sliced cucumbers and chopped tomatoes.

MARIAN'S POT ROAST   *8 servings*

Sometimes I serve pot roast with noodles. I usually slice the meat, pour the gravy over it, and then surround it with noodles. Chopped parsley or caraway seeds sprinkled over the noodles gives a little bit of zip to the dish.

6 medium onions, chopped
2 tablespoons shortening
6 pounds brisket of beef or
  5 pounds boneless chuck
salt and pepper

1 cup chili sauce
2 tablespoons lemon juice
2 tablespoons brown sugar
1 10½-ounce can tomato soup

Sauté onions in shortening until golden. Set aside. • In heavy pot brown on all sides brisket or chuck. • Sprinkle meat with salt and pepper. Cover tightly and bake slowly for 2½ to 3 hours at 300 degrees. Then add the rest of the ingredients, including the onions. • If you wish, freeze at this point. When ready to serve, defrost and cook another half hour. Reheat at serving time.

And they, continuing daily with one accord in the temple, and breaking bread from house to house, did eat their meat with gladness and singleness of heart, Praising God, and having favour with all the people. And the Lord added to the church daily such as should be saved (Acts 2:46–47).

POTATO SOUFFLÉ *8 servings*

1 6½-ounce package instant mashed potatoes
6 eggs, separated
½ cup heavy cream
¼ teaspoon nutmeg
1 teaspoon salt

2¼ cups grated Swiss cheese
3 tablespoons grated onion
½ cup bread crumbs
4 tablespoons butter
2 tablespoons grated Parmesan cheese

Cook potatoes according to directions on package; cool. • Beat egg yolks; add cream, nutmeg, salt, cheese, and onion. Combine with cooled potatoes. • Beat egg whites until stiff. Fold mixture into stiffly beaten egg whites. • Pour into two 2-quart soufflé dishes. Top each with ½ of the bread crumbs, butter, and grated Parmesan cheese. Bake at 350 degrees for 40 to 45 minutes. • This soufflé may be frozen and then baked to serve.

VEGETABLE SALAD   *9 servings*

1 3-ounce package lemon
  gelatin
½ cup boiling water
1 cup mayonnaise
¼ cup liquid from peas
¼ cup vinegar
1 tablespoon granulated sugar
1 teaspoon salt

1 tablespoon green pepper,
  chopped
1 tablespoon onion, chopped
1 teaspoon prepared mustard
2 cups canned peas, drained
1 cup diced cooked carrots
1 cup celery, chopped

Dissolve gelatin in boiling water. Cool. Add mayonnaise. Add all remaining ingredients. Pour into 9 x 9-inch glass dish. Refrigerate.

LEMON RIBBON-LAYERED MERINGUE PIE
6 to 8 servings

6 tablespoons butter
grated peel of 1 lemon
⅓ cup lemon juice
⅛ teaspoon salt
1 cup granulated sugar

2 whole eggs plus 2 yolks
1 quart vanilla ice cream
1 baked 9-inch pastry shell
3 egg whites
6 tablespoons sugar

To make the lemon-butter sauce, melt butter, add lemon peel, lemon juice, salt, and the 1 cup of sugar. Slightly beat whole eggs with egg yolks; combine eggs with the other mixture and cook over boiling water, beating constantly with a whisk until thick and smooth. Cool. • Smooth half of the ice cream in pastry shell; freeze. • Spread over it half of the cooled lemon-butter; freeze. • Cover with other half of ice cream; freeze. • Top with remaining lemon butter; freeze. • Beat egg whites until stiff, gradually beating in 6 tablespoons sugar; spread meringue on pie. • Place pie on board; lightly brown in a 475 degree oven. Serve immediately or freeze.

A tossed green salad—the perfect opportunity for an
imaginative combination of flavor, color, and texture

An attractive buffet setting requires advance planning
not only of menu but serving dishes too

WELCOME TO NEW MINISTER

And how hear without someone to spread the news? And how could anyone spread the news without a commission to do so? And that is what Scripture affirms: "How welcome are the feet of the messengers of good news!" (Romans 10:14–15, NEB).

The new minister cannot be expected to remember each face and name immediately, but it would be nice for him to know in some way that you welcome him. A dinner given by the church in honor of the new minister would be an appropriate way to welcome him and his family.

FOR SUMMER:

Tomato Juice
*Mary Jane's Cheese Balls
Sliced Turkey and Ham
*Egg Bread
*Party Salad
"Welcome" Sheetcake from
Bakery
Coffee   Tea

FOR WINTER:

Grapefruit Juice
*Pork Creole with Noodles
Buttered Peas
*Egg Bread
Celery and Carrot Sticks
"Welcome" Sheetcake from
Bakery
Coffee   Tea

A "welcome" sheet-cake from the bakery is a simple way to solve the dessert problem for a large crowd. Decorated and surrounded by low flowers and greenery from the yard, it can also serve as a "welcome" centerpiece for the buffet table.

MARY JANE'S CHEESE BALLS

About 24 balls

Make appetizers as pretty as possible, for as openers to any get-together they set the scene; even if their appearance is brief, they are extremely important.

1 5-ounce jar sharp cheese ½ cup unsifted flour
¼ cup butter ½ teaspoon salt

Cream cheese and butter; sift flour and salt over cheese mixture. Mix well. Roll into small balls and place on greased cookie sheet. • Chill overnight (at least 8 hours). • Bake in preheated 400 degree oven for 10 minutes or until golden brown. Serve hot. • These may be frozen before baking.

EGG BREAD   *2 loaves*

2 cakes compressed, or ½ cup melted butter or
    2 packages active dry yeast   margarine
½ cup warm, not hot, water 1 cup evaporated milk
2 eggs ½ cup hot water
½ cup sugar 1½ teaspoons salt
5 cups unsifted flour

Soak yeast in warm water. (For compressed yeast use lukewarm water; for dry yeast use 90 degree water.) • Beat eggs in large mixing bowl; beat in sugar. Add melted butter, evaporated milk, hot water, and salt. Mix well. • Be sure mixture is only lukewarm. Add yeast. Add 1 cup unsifted flour. Beat until smooth. If using mixer, add all the remaining flour, while mixing at low speed, and use a rubber spatula to scrape dough from sides of bowl. When dough is elastic and rides up around top of beaters, it is kneaded enough. Or you may beat in same amount of flour by hand. • Turn on floured board and knead lightly until satiny. Put into greased bowl. Cover dough and allow to rise in warm place until double in bulk. Turn onto lightly floured board, cut in half, and mold into two loaves. • To braid—divide each loaf into 3 equal parts. Roll with hands and braid, starting from the middle of the loaf and working toward each end so that the loaf is thicker in the middle and tapers toward the ends. • Place on greased jelly roll pan and again allow to rise until double in bulk. • Bake at 375 degrees for 15 minutes, and then turn oven temperature down to 350 and bake 40 more minutes, or until loaf sounds hollow when thumped with knuckles. • Turn out on rack, brush with butter, and let cool away from drafts. This bread does not need reheating for serving.

PARTY SALAD   *12 servings*

LOWER LAYER:

1 6-ounce box lemon gelatin
2 cups boiling water
2 cups cold water

1 No. 2 can pineapple tidbits
2 large bananas, sliced
10 marshmallows, cut in pieces

Dissolve gelatin in boiling water. Stir in cold water. Chill until slightly thickened. Add drained **pineapple** (save juice), sliced bananas, and marshmallow pieces. Pour into 9 x 13-inch dish; chill until firm.

TOPPING:

1 cup pineapple juice
2 tablespoons flour
1 egg, beaten
½ cup sugar

2 tablespoons butter
1 cup heavy cream, whipped
2 tablespoons powdered sugar
½ cup grated cheddar cheese

Combine pineapple juice, flour, egg, and sugar. Cook, stirring constantly until thick. Then add 2 tablespoons butter. • Let cool; then fold in cream, whipped and sweetened with powdered sugar. • Spread over first layer and sprinkle grated cheese over the top. Chill and cut into squares.

And this I pray, that your love may abound yet more and more in knowledge and in all judgment (Philippians 1:9).

PORK CREOLE WITH NOODLES
50 *servings*

Pasta dishes are valued for entertaining as they can be prepared ahead of time. They are most attractive served in casseroles for buffets and informal dining.

9 pounds pork shoulder,
   ½-inch cubes
4½ cups celery, ½-inch
   diagonal slices
3 cups onions, finely chopped
1½ cups green pepper,
   chopped in 1-inch cubes
1½ pounds mushrooms, sliced
2½ quarts tomato sauce

1½ quarts water
3⅓ tablespoons salt
½ tablespoon black pepper
¾ cup parsley, chopped
3 tablespoons Worcestershire
   sauce
4½ quarts cooked noodles,
   (approx. 4 12-ounce packages)

Cut pork into cubes and put into two 20 x 12 x 2½-inch pans; brown in 325 degree oven for 45 minutes. • Drain off excess fat. Add celery, onion, green pepper, and mushrooms to pork cubes; cover and cook in oven until tender, about 1 hour. • Mix together tomato sauce, water, salt, pepper, parsley, and Worcestershire sauce; pour over meat and vegetable ingredients. • Arrange cooked noodles and meat mixture in alternate layers, using the two above size pans. • Cover and bake 1 hour in 350 degree oven.

SENIOR CITIZEN DINNER

Cast me not off in the time of old age; forsake me not when my strength faileth (Psalm 71:9).

In today's mobile society more and more people are finding themselves away "from the old homestead." Thus, the retirement centers must fill a need in the lives of aging parents. Many churches have established retirement centers in an effort to fill a social need. While children may be very able and willing to care for aging parents, the senior citizen somehow seems more secure in a town where he or she has lived for most of his or her years. To invite some of these senior citizens into your home to share a Sunday dinner with your family might bring untold happiness to them and to your own family.

*Chicken and Sea Shells   Herbed Tomato Juice

*Asparagus Salad   *Wanda's Hot Chicken Salad

*Dilled Carrots   *Spiced Baked Rhubarb

Butter Rolls   Hot Muffins

*Jan Coe's Custard

Milk   Tea   Coffee

These menus are intentionally bland in consideration for the diets of senior citizens. Serve the chicken and sea shells in pretty bright oven-to-table casseroles. Add other color to the table with bright linens and fresh flowers.

37

Sea shell macaroni has beome one of my favorite pastas; it is a little easier to eat and more interesting to look at than plain spaghetti. And there seem to be more and more new pastas on the market every day that you can use for a change from the familiar ones.

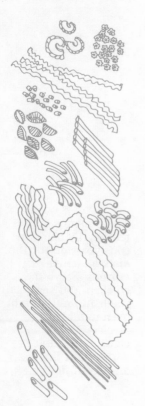

4- to 5-pound stewing chicken, cooked, boned, and cut into small pieces
broth from chicken
½ pound small sea shell macaroni, boiled until tender
¾ cup grated cheddar cheese
1 cup tomato juice
2 cups chopped celery

1 cup chopped onion
1 cup ripe olives, cut in small pieces
2 4-ounce cans mushrooms, stems and pieces, drained
1 10-ounce package frozen peas, cooked and drained
salt and pepper to taste

Combine ½ cup chicken broth, tomato juice, celery, and onion in saucepan and boil until celery and onion are tender. Mix all ingredients; season to taste with salt and pepper. If it seems too dry, add more chicken broth. • Put in two 2-quart casseroles and cover. • Bake 1½ hours in 325 degree oven.

ASPARAGUS SALAD   *1 serving*

¼ cup lettuce
3 to 5 stalks canned asparagus spears

mayonnaise
parsley

For each individual serving: shred ¼ cup lettuce; place on salad plate. Arrange chilled canned asparagus spears on top. Garnish with sprig of parsley and mayonnaise on side of plate.

DILLED CARROTS   *8 servings*

2 10-ounce packages frozen
  carrots
1 teaspoon sugar

1 tablespoon butter
1 teaspoon dill weed

Cook 2 packages of frozen carrots according to directions, adding 1 teaspoon of sugar to the water. Drain; add 1 tablespoon
butter and 1 teaspoon dill weed. Mix until butter and dill weed
coat all of the carrots. Serve hot.

The carrot always
wins praise for its
rich hue. Orange is
sometimes described
as the most "edible"
color.

Rebuke not an elder, but entreat him as a father; and the
younger men as brethren (1 Timothy 5:1).

JAN COE'S CUSTARD   *8 servings*

4 cups milk, scalded
6 eggs
¼ teaspoon salt

2 teaspoon vanilla extract
½ cup sugar

Beat eggs, sugar, salt, and vanilla. Combine with scalded milk
and *strain* into 8 custard cups. • Place custard cups in a pan of
water and bake at 325 degrees for 40 minutes. • Chill.

Hearken unto thy father that begat thee, and despise not thy
mother when she is old (Proverbs 23:22).

WANDA'S HOT CHICKEN SALAD
6 *servings*

2 cups cooked chicken, diced
¼ cup chicken bouillon
1 cup mayonnaise
2 tablespoons lemon juice
2 tablespoons grated onion
1½ cups celery, thinly sliced

1 cup slivered almonds
1 pimiento, sliced in strips
salt and pepper to taste
6 ramekins or hollowed
  grapefruit halves
¾ cup crushed potato chips
½ cup grated American cheese

Heat diced chicken and bouillon over low heat in covered saucepan until hot. Remove from heat. • Blend mayonnaise, lemon juice, and grated onion together. To bouillon add the celery, almonds, pimiento, and mayonnaise, tossing with forks. Season with salt and pepper to taste. • Fill shells. Sprinkle tops with crushed potato chips and grated cheese. • Bake at 400 degrees for 20 minutes or until hot through.

SPICED BAKED RHUBARB   8 *servings*

4 cups rhubarb, cut in ½-inch
  pieces
1½ cups sugar
½ teaspoon cinnamon

½ teaspoon mace
6 whole cloves
1 orange, juice and grated peel

Wash rhubarb and cut without peeling. In mixing bowl combine rhubarb with remaining ingredients. • Remove to buttered baking dish. Cover and bake for 30 minutes in 350 degree oven. Serve hot or chilled.

THE CHURCH CONVENTION

So the Twelve called the whole body of disciples together and said, "It would be a grave mistake for us to neglect the word of God in order to wait at table. Therefore, friends, *look out seven men* of good reputation from your number, men full of the Spirit and of wisdom, and we will appoint them to deal with these matters, while we devote ourselves to prayer and to the ministry of the Word." This proposal proved acceptable to the whole body. They elected Stephen, a man full of faith and of the Holy Spirit, Philip, Prochorus, Nicanor, Timon, Parmenas, and Nicolas of Antioch, a former convert to Judaism. These they presented to the apostles, who prayed and laid their hands on them.

The word of God now spread more and more widely; the number of disciples in Jerusalem went on increasing rapidly, and very many of the priests adhered to the Faith (Acts 6: 2–7, NEB, italics mine).

For a long time, people in many walks of life have used food as a means of creating a happy atmosphere in which differences can be discussed. The church convention usually deals with many diverse thoughts. How often disagreements can take on a different attitude over the meal together! The following are some recipes which can be used to feed a crowd, in or out of the church hall. An excellent way to prepare a quantity of food is to appoint a Committee of Seven to cook up one, two, or three portions of food for 12 to 24 people. This provides for greater participation and in some cases a tastier product than food cooked in larger batches.

Serve apple juice in a variety of brightly colored paper cups. These can be purchased from most paper supply houses in large cities. If you get a supply of these to keep on hand, they really make a pretty tray.

Apple Juice

*_Sesame Twists_

*_Glazed Ham Rolls or_

*_Ground Beef and Noodles_

Tossed Vegetable Salad with Assorted Dressings

Buttered Rolls

*_Joan's Peppermint Pudding_

Coffee   Tea

SESAME TWISTS

4½ cups sifted flour	2 eggs
3 teaspoons baking powder	1 cup toasted sesame seeds
½ teaspoon salt	½ teaspoon grated lemon rind
1 cup (2 sticks) margarine	2 tablespoons water
1½ cups sugar	2 tablespoons lemon juice

Sift flour, baking powder, and salt together. Cream margarine and sugar until light and fluffy. Beat in eggs; then stir in ⅓ cup toasted sesame seeds and the lemon rind. Add the flour mixture alternately with the water and lemon juice. • Chill. • Divide dough into 8 equal parts. Roll each part into a strip 24 inches long; cut strip into 6 pieces. • Along one side at ½-inch intervals, cut slits halfway through each piece. Place on greased baking sheet, coiling ends toward the center of uncut side. Sprinkle with remaining sesame seeds. • Bake in preheated 400 degree oven for 10 to 12 minutes. These may be baked the day before and reheated at time of serving.

GLAZED HAM ROLLS   *10 servings*

1 pound fresh pork, ground
2 pounds ground ham
¼ pound bread crumbs, dried,
   about 1 cup

1 cup milk
3 eggs, beaten
¼ teaspoon salt

Mix all ingredients until blended. Form into 10 or more rolls; bake in oven at 350 degrees for 45 minutes. • Pour off excess juice and fat.

GLAZE:

1 cup brown sugar
¾ teaspoon ginger
⅛ teaspoon cinnamon

⅛ teaspoon nutmeg
pinch of salt
1 cup orange juice

Boil glaze ingredients together for a few minutes. Pour over all rolls and bake for 45 minutes more at 350 degrees, basting occasionally.

GROUND BEEF AND NOODLES
serves 8

1 8-ounce package noodles,
   (curly)
2 tablespoons salad oil
1½ pounds ground chuck
2 medium onions, chopped
1 green pepper, chopped
1 1-pound, 12-ounce can whole
   kernel corn

1 tablespoon Worcestershire
   sauce
2 10¾-ounce cans cream of
   tomato soup
1 16-ounce can stewed
   tomatoes
½ pound cheese, cut in cubes
salt and pepper to taste

Cook noodles according to directions on package. • Brown meat, onions, and green pepper in oil. Add remaining ingredients. Adjust seasoning, adding salt and pepper to taste. • Combine with cooked noodles. Pour into 3-quart casserole with cover. • Bake 3 hours at 300 degrees.

It is God himself who called you to share in the life of his Son Jesus Christ our Lord; and God keeps faith. I appeal to you, my brothers, in the name of our Lord Jesus Christ: agree among yourselves, and avoid divisions; be firmly joined in unity of mind and thought (1 Corinthians 1:5–10, NEB).

JOAN'S PEPPERMINT PUDDING　　*6 servings*

1½ cups chocolate wafers, crushed
⅓ cup butter
1 envelope unflavored gelatin
4 tablespoons cold water
½ cup scalded milk

½ cup sugar
1 pint whipping cream
1 teaspoon peppermint extract
few drops of green coloring
maraschino cherries

Make crumb crust from wafers and butter. Mix well and line square pan. Chill. (Crust may be made day ahead.) • Soak gelatin in cold water and add to milk. Dissolve sugar in milk and gelatin mixture. • Let cool, but don't let mixture get too cold—about tepid. • Whip cream and add flavoring and coloring. Mix with gelatin mixture. • Pour into crumb crust and sprinkle top with crushed wafers. Garnish with maraschino cherries. • Chill overnight. When doubling this recipe, go easy on flavoring.

LOVE BASKETS

I showed you that it is our duty to help the weak in this way, by hard work, and that we should keep in mind the words of the Lord Jesus, who himself said, "Happiness lies more in giving than in receiving" (Acts 20:35, NEB).

In the years before the Great Depression, the rule of the day was, "It is more blessed to give than to receive." In these days of our great abundance, should we not rekindle this philosophy? Some religious communities provide for the less fortunate of their members, but, in turn, those who receive are those who at a future date become givers in time, material, or money. Those receiving look toward better days and never consider their condition a permanent one. They receive the "love baskets" in the spirit with which they are given—in the spirit of Christian love! For some reason, today many are allowing the government to assume the responsibility of taking care of our less fortunate brethren—the government has become "our brother's keeper" when we, the Christian community, should be our brother's brother.

Religion that is pure and genuine in the sight of God the Father will show itself by such things as visiting orphans and widows in their distress (James 1:27, Phillips).

SUGGESTIONS FOR LOVE BASKETS

A love basket for the poor could include:

Ten Dollar Bill—for something which they might need to buy themselves.

A *Simplified Version of the Bible*—because we "cannot live by bread alone."

A *Basket of Food Stuffs* which would contain the following:

A *Ham* which can be cooked and prepared later.

A *Turkey* which you have cooked and prepared or

Dad's Old-Fashioned Stew

Canned Goods which would go with the turkey such as *cranberry sauce, peas, sweet potatoes.*

Fruits for a salad.

A love basket for the sick could include:

Chicken Soup
Crackers
Gelatin Salad
Pound Cake

> For just as you have many members in one physical body and those members differ in their functions, so we, though many in number, compose one body in Christ and are all members of one another. Through the grace of God we have different gifts. If our gift is preaching, let us preach to the limit of our vision. If it is serving others let us concentrate on our service; if it is teaching let us give all we have to our teaching; and if our gift be the stimulating of the faith of others let us set ourselves to it. Let the man who is called to give, give freely; let the man who wields authority think of his responsibility; and let the man who feels sympathy for his fellows act cheerfully (Romans 12:4–8, Phillips).

DAD'S OLD-FASHIONED STEW   *Serves 8*

2 pounds beef chuck, cut in 1½-inch cubes
2 tablespoons salad oil
1 chopped onion
clove of garlic
4 cups boiling water
1 tablespoon salt
1 tablespoon lemon juice
1 teaspoon sugar
1 teaspoon Worcestershire sauce
½ teaspoon pepper
½ teaspoon paprika
a bay leaf or two
dash of allspice or cloves
6 carrots cut in quarters
1 pound small white onions
1 cup diced raw potatoes

Heat 2 tablespoons fat in dutch oven. Add 2 pounds beef chuck, cut in 1½-inch cubes, and brown on all sides—keep turning the cubes (use tongs). Don't hurry—this should take about 20 minutes. Add chopped onion, a clove of garlic (on toothpick so you can retrieve it), 4 cups boiling water, 1 tablespoon each salt and lemon juice, 1 teaspoon each sugar and Worcestershire sauce, ½ teaspoon each pepper and paprika, a bay leaf or two, and a dash of allspice or cloves.

Gentle cooking is what makes the meat tender; so cover and simmer (not boil) 2 hours. Stir now and then to prevent sticking. • When meat is almost done, add the vegetables—6 carrots cut in quarters, 1 pound peeled small white onions, and diced potatoes. • Simmer the stew 30 minutes longer or until everything in the kettle is tender. Discard bay leaf and garlic.

To make gravy, pour ½ cup cold water into a shaker and then add ¼ cup flour; shake hard to blend. • Remove the stew from heat, push meat and vegetables to one side of pan, stir in flour mixture. Cook and stir until gravy thickens and boils. Cook gently a few minutes.

It is the browning—long and lazy—that gives a stew the rich color and flavor men like.

CHICKEN SOUP

1 5-pound stewing chicken, cut into pieces	2 ribs of celery
3 quarts water	1 sprig parsley
1 medium onion, stuffed with 3 whole cloves	1 10-ounce package of frozen mixed vegetables
1 carrot	salt to taste
	pepper to taste

Bring water to boil; add cut up chicken, onion, carrot, celery, and parsley. When water boils again, turn to simmer and cook 3 hours or until meat is tender. • Strain broth; fill a thermos bottle with part of it. • Add boned chicken and mixed vegetables to remaining broth; boil for five minutes and remove from heat. A thermos bottle full of soup should be enough for the member of the family who is ill. The rest of the soup with vegetables should feed the family.

Heal the sick, raise the dead, cleanse lepers, cast out devils. You received without cost; give without charge (Matthew 10:8, NEB).

But if a man has enough to live on, and yet when he sees his brother in need shuts up his heart against him, how can it be said that the divine love dwells in him?

My children, love must not be a matter of words or talk; it must be genuine, and show itself in action (1 John 3:17–18, NEB).

Chicken soup with mixed vegetables—a hearty meal
(recipe, page 48)

POUND CAKE *16 generous servings*

2 cups butter (4 sticks)
2 cups granulated sugar
8 eggs, or 2 cups
2 teaspoons vanilla extract
4 cups sifted cake flour
¼ teaspoon salt

1½ cups candied pineapple, diced
1½ cups candied cherries, diced
½ cup flaked coconut

Have all ingredients at about 75 degrees. • Preheat oven to 300 degrees. Grease 9- or 10-inch tube pan or 2 loaf pans. • Cream butter until very creamy (several minutes) with electric mixer. Add sugar and cream until mixture is fluffy and light (about 10 to 12 minutes in mixer), pushing down around sides of bowl and up from bottom of bowl with rubber spatula. • Add eggs, one at a time, beating well after each addition (about 1 minute after each). Add vanilla. • Sift flour with salt and add to mixture all at once, folding in with as little stirring as possible. (In mixer, use lowest speed.) • Flour pineapple and cherries lightly. Fold pineapple, cherries, and coconut gently into batter. • Pour into greased pan and bake in slow oven at 300 degrees for about 1½ hours. Test for doneness in center of cake with tip of finger.

When I was hungry, you gave me food; when thirsty, you gave me drink; when I was a stranger you took me into your home, when naked you clothed me; when I was ill you came to my help, when in prison you visited me (Matthew 25: 36–37).

WOMEN'S MISSIONARY CIRCLE

And these were His gifts: some to be apostles, some prophets, some evangelists, some pastors and teachers, to equip God's people for work in his service, to the building up of the body of Christ. So shall we all at last attain to the unity inherent in our faith and our knowledge of the Son of God—to mature manhood, measured by nothing less than the full stature of Christ (Ephesians 4:11–13, NEB).

Some of us by our supportive work at home help those who are out teaching. If you are chosen to be the Martha of the Missionary Circle, here are some suggested refreshments to help keep the workers sustained and to enhance their time of fellowship before, during, or after the meeting.

*Chicken Salad
*Cheese Puffs
*Nell's Orange Jewel Cookies
Coffee   Tea

*Swiss Onion Pie
Frosted Fruit Cups
Mints
Coffee   Tea

*Tuna Salad Sandwiches
*Marilyn's Apple Cake
Coffee   Tea

I like to serve my chicken salad on green salad plates because you do not need as much lettuce, a real help when lettuce is very expensive.

Get colored mints to complement your table linens and your flowers; this also adds to the color of the day.

CHICKEN SALAD   *8 servings*

Another attractive way to serve the chicken salad is in cantaloupe or honey-dew rings placed on lettuce leaves. Be careful to refrigerate chicken salad if it is made in advance.

3 cups cooked chicken, diced
½ cup celery, thinly sliced
2 cups canned pineapple tidbits, drained
½ cup slivered blanched almonds

1 cup mayonnaise
1 teaspoon salt
pepper to taste
8 peach halves
lettuce and parsley

Combine chicken, celery, pineapple and almonds with mayonnaise until completely mixed. Season with salt and pepper to taste. Chill. Scoop onto chilled peach half. Serve in lettuce cups and garnish with parsley.

CHEESE PUFFS   *30 puffs*

1 can refrigerator biscuits
peanut oil

¼ pound cheddar cheese, cubed into 30 pieces

Remove biscuits from container. Separate and cut each biscuit into thirds. Wrap each piece around a cube of cheddar cheese to form small balls. • Fry in deep hot oil, 385 degrees, until golden brown. Drain on paper towels. Serve hot.

NELL'S ORANGE JEWEL COOKIES   *4 dozen*

1⅓ cups (12 ounces) jellied orange candy slices
1½ cups sifted flour
1 teaspoon baking powder
½ teaspoon salt
⅔ cup shortening

⅔ cup granulated sugar
⅔ cup brown sugar, packed
1 egg
1 teaspoon vanilla extract
1½ cups quick-cooking oats
1 3½-ounce can coconut

Preheat oven to 375 degrees. Grease cookie sheets. • Cut jellied orange slices into small pieces. Sift together flour, baking powder, salt. Cream together shortening and sugars. Beat in egg and vanilla. Stir in sifted ingredients. Add oats, coconut, and cut candy. Mix well. • Shape into very small balls using rounded tablespoons of dough. Place on greased cookie sheets and flatten slightly. • Bake 10 to 12 minutes.

Then He said to them: "Go forth to every part of the world, and proclaim the Good News to the whole creation" (Mark 16:15, NEB).

SWISS ONION PIE   *6 servings*

3 cups Spanish onions, thinly sliced
3 tablespoons butter
6 slices bacon
2 eggs

1 tablespoon flour
½ cup milk
½ teaspoon salt
1½ cups sour cream
1 9-inch pastry shell

Cook onions gently in butter until tender and clear in appearance. Set aside to cool. • Fry bacon to the not-quite-done stage. Drain on paper toweling. Cut into 1-inch lengths. • With fork whip the eggs in mixing bowl until blended. Combine the flour with 2 tablespoons milk, mixing until smooth. Add flour mixture to the eggs along with the remaining milk, salt, and sour cream. Mix well. • Spoon the onions into the chilled unbaked pastry shell. Pour custard mixture over onions. Top pie with bacon pieces. • Bake in 400 degree oven until firm—about 35 minutes. Serve at once. This pie may be served as a main course, appetizer, or meat partner.

The problem of serving unexpected guests or of finding yourself out of necessary ingredients is minimized if you can keep ample supplies on hand. I keep ground beef and other frequently used meats on hand in the freezer, and I like to buy canned fruits by the case. The burden is less when two or three neighbors share in making quantity purchases.

TUNA SALAD SANDWICHES   *8 servings*

8 hamburger buns, split   cheese
2 cups tuna salad

Spread each half hamburger bun with your favorite tuna salad spread. Top with sliced or grated cheese; broil until cheese is melted. Garnish with pickles and potato chips on plate. Serve immediately.

There is no distinction between Jew and Greek, because the same Lord is Lord of all, and is rich enough for the need of all who invoke him (Romans 10:12, NEB).

MARILYN'S APPLE CAKE   *12 servings*

2 cans apple pie filling   ½ cup blanched slivered
1 teaspoon cinnamon   almonds
1 box yellow cake mix   ½ cup (1 stick) butter or
                                    margarine
                                 whipping cream or ice cream

Pour apple pie filling into 9 x 13-inch greased baking dish. Sprinkle with cinnamon. Sprinkle dry cake mix over apples; sprinkle almonds over cake mix. Spoon melted butter over all. • Bake at 350 degrees for 45 minutes. Serve with whipped cream or soft ice cream.

MOTHER–DAUGHTER TEA

Proverbs 31:10–30 paints a beautiful picture of the godly woman. What a fine tribute to a mother when "her children arise up, and call her blessed; her husband also, and he praiseth her." A Mother-Daughter Tea can be an expression of the love, respect, and honor that you have for your mother.

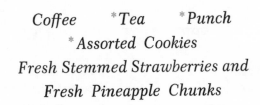

Coffee   **Tea*   **Punch*
*Assorted Cookies
Fresh Stemmed Strawberries and
Fresh Pineapple Chunks

Who can find a virtuous woman? for her price is far above rubies. The heart of her husband doth safely trust in her, so that he shall have no need of spoil. She will do him good and not evil all the days of her life. She seeketh wool, and flax, and worketh willingly with her hands. She is like the merchants' ships; she bringeth her food from afar. She riseth also while it is yet night, and giveth meat to her household, and a portion to her maidens. She considereth a field, and buyeth it: with the fruit of her hands she planteth a vineyard. She girdeth her loins with strength, and strengtheneth

In the Old South, the pineapple, greatly loved by the people, was carved above the door as a symbol of hospitality. A fruit bowl of bite-sized chunks of fully ripened fresh pineapple is beautiful with strawberries as a vivid color contrast. Provide toothpicks for guests to pick up the fruit and bowls of sugar for dipping it: brown sugar for the pineapple and powdered sugar for the strawberries.

her arms. She perceiveth that her merchandise is good: her candle goeth not out by night. She layeth her hands to the spindle, and her hands hold the distaff. She stretcheth out her hand to the poor; yea, she reacheth forth her hands to the needy. She is not afraid of the snow for her household: for all her household are clothed with scarlet. She maketh herself coverings of tapestry; her clothing is silk and purple. Her husband is known in the gates, when he sitteth among the elders of the land. She maketh fine linen, and selleth it; and delivereth girdles unto the merchant. Strength and honour are her clothing and she shall rejoice in time to come. She openeth her mouth with wisdom; and in her tongue is the law of kindness. She looketh well to the ways of her household, and eateth not the bread of idleness. Her children arise up, and call her blessed; her husband also, and he praiseth her (Proverbs 31:10–28).

SPICY HOT TEA PUNCH *Serves 35*

5 quarts water
4 cups sugar
2 tablespoons whole cloves
1 3-inch piece cinnamon stick
1 tablespoon whole allspice

6 tea bags
1 cup pineapple juice
⅔ cup lemon juice (about 3 lemons)
1 cup orange juice (about 3 oranges)

The canny hostess will have additional platters ready to replace those on the table when the trays become ragged looking. Medium-size rather than large platters are easier to keep trim.

Combine 1 quart of the water, sugar, and spices and bring to a boil. Reduce heat and simmer 5 minutes; strain. • Bring 1 quart of the water to a boil and pour over tea bags; steep five minutes. Combine with spice mixture and juices. • Boil the remaining 3 quarts of water and add to above mixture. • Refrigerate unused portion and reheat as needed.

NOTE: Make 4 recipes to serve about 150 people.

STRAWBERRY FESTIVAL TEA *Serves 20*

1 quart fresh strawberries
1⅓ cups sugar

1 gallon tea, cooled
2 6-ounce cans frozen
  lemonade

In the morning, check all the details for the party. Has the ice been made? Have the necessary serving pieces been gathered?

Clean and hull strawberries. Slice in half and stir in sugar. • Make 1 gallon tea; cool. • Mix with frozen lemonade concentrate; add strawberries. Serve over ice ring in punch bowl or over ice in tall glasses.

LIME SHERBET PUNCH
Serves about 100

12 quarts lemon-lime soda   6 quarts lime sherbet

Into a 3-gallon punch bowl, put a large piece of ice. Pour in 4 quarts of lemon-lime soda and 2 quarts lime sherbet. Makes 3 punch bowls full.

LOIS'S EGG YOLK COOKIES *3 dozen*

4 yolks of hard-boiled eggs
1 pound butter or margarine
2 cups granulated sugar
4½ cups unsifted cake flour

8 teaspoons lemon juice
grated rind of 1 lemon
1 teaspoon vanilla extract
3 dozen candied cherries

Put hard-boiled egg yolks through fine sieve. Cream butter; add sugar, flour, egg yolks, lemon juice, grated lemon rind, and vanilla. Mix thoroughly. • Chill. • Shape into marble-sized balls and press together into triangles. Press whole candied cherry into center. • Bake on greased cookie sheets for about 20 minutes at 300 degrees or until slightly brown around the edges. Cool and store in tight container. These may also be frozen.

"Honour your father and mother" is the first commandment with a promise attached, in the words: "that it may be well with you and that you may live long in the land" (Ephesians 6:23, NEB).

COCOA-NUT BARS

½ cup soft butter (1 stick)	½ cup finely chopped walnuts
¼ cup sugar	¼ cup butter (½ stick)
5 tablespoons cocoa	6 tablespoons milk
1 teaspoon vanilla extract	1 package chocolate pudding
1 egg, slightly beaten	mix
3 cups soda cracker crumbs	2 cups sifted powdered sugar
(about 28 crackers)	2 1-ounce squares semi-sweet
1 cup finely grated coconut	chocolate
	1 tablespoon butter

Put first five ingredients into top of double boiler. Set over boiling water and stir until smooth. • Add cracker crumbs, coconut, and walnuts. Stir until blended. • Cream together the butter, milk, pudding mix, and powdered sugar; add to first mixture. • Over low heat, melt the chocolate with the tablespoon of butter until blended and smooth. Stir this into mixture. • Roll into balls and sprinkle with confectioners' sugar. Put into paper bon-bon cups.

VISITING MINISTER
OR CHURCH OFFICIAL

In a word, accept one another as Christ accepted us, to the glory of God. I mean that Christ became a servant of the Jewish people to maintain the truth of God by making good his promises to the patriarchs, and at the same time to give the Gentiles cause to glorify God for his mercy (Romans 15:7–8, NEB).

How better to give your pastor time off than to invite a church official, a layman, or a friend of the pastor's to preach and teach on a Sunday? A reception before the evening service can provide just enough of a snack for those who have eaten early and not too much for those who have eaten late. Be sure to have variety with your "Pastors' Punch."

Chinese Egg Rolls
Sweet and Sour Meatballs
Tuna-Filled Puffs
Bankers' Oatmeal Cookies
Pastors' Punch
Mints
Tea   Coffee

CHINESE EGG ROLLS

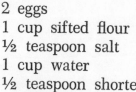

Serve egg rolls with soy sauce, Chinese sweet-sour sauce, or Chinese mustard. Egg rolls may also be served as the main dish at a luncheon.

2 eggs
1 cup sifted flour
½ teaspoon salt
1 cup water
½ teaspoon shortening or cooking oil
2 tablespoons raw carrot, shredded
2 tablespoons raw celery, shredded

1 tablespoon finely diced scallions
½ cup cooked meat (choice of pork, beef, chicken, ham)
1 teaspoon salt
½ cup shrimp, cooked
dash of pepper
2 teaspoons oil or other fat
1 teaspoon granulated sugar

Beat eggs. Stir in flour and ½ teaspoon salt alternately with water to make thin batter. Save a little batter for sealing the rolls later. • Heat a frying pan over moderate heat and melt in it shortening (not butter) or cooking oil. Pour enough batter to make a thin pancake and cook the pancake on one side for only 1 minute. • Remove the pancake from the pan and put it on a flat surface which has been warmed. Use up the rest of the batter in the same way. • Let the pancakes cool and prepare this filling: Shred enough raw carrot and raw celery to make 2 tablespoons each. Cook these vegetables in a little boiling water for about 4 minutes; then drain and place them in a mixing bowl. • Allow to cool, then add finely diced scallions. • Chop the meat very finely—cooked pork, beef, chicken, or ham—and add 1 teaspoon salt, chopped shrimp, pepper, 2 teaspoons oil, and sugar. Combine the two mixtures and mix well. • In the middle of each cooled pancake, place 1 generous teaspoon of the vegetable-meat mixture. Roll the pancakes, folding in the ends while rolling, and seal the rolls with the remaining egg batter. Fry the pancakes in a pan containing 2 inches of oil at a moderate temperature, 350 to 365 degrees. Cook the pancakes to a golden brown on one side for about 15 minutes; then turn them to brown the other side. Remove from the pan; drain on absorbent paper and serve hot. These may be frozen. Before serving heat for 10 minutes in 400 degree oven.

SWEET AND SOUR MEATBALLS
36 to 40 meatballs

1 pound ground pork,
   unseasoned
2 pounds ground round beef
½ medium onion, finely grated
1 teaspoon salt

2 eggs, slightly beaten
¼ cup water
1 tablespoon curry powder
½ teaspoon nutmeg
3 tablespoons butter

Mix salt into egg. Combine all ingredients until thoroughly mixed. Form into 1½-inch balls. Brown in 3 tablespoons of butter in 10-inch skillet. • Transfer the browned meatballs to a 3-quart covered baking dish. Bake at 325 degrees for about 1 hour. • Cook with sauce for additional 30 minutes:

SAUCE:

½ cup water
1 tablespoon cornstarch
2 tablespoons sugar
3 tablespoons vinegar
   (white)

1 tablespoon soy sauce
1 can (#2) pineapple chunks
   with syrup.
grated coconut

Combine all sauce ingredients except coconut. Cook sauce at medium heat while browning meatballs. Combine with meatballs as above. Garnish with grated coconut.

61

TUNA-FILLED PUFFS

CHEF GEORGE'S PUFF SHELLS:

Puff shells may also be filled with highly seasoned creamed seafood or chicken or a thick sharp cheese sauce. These may be filled and frozen. Take directly from freezer to oven to party table.

2 cups water
1 cup butter
2⅔ cups flour

10 whole eggs
½ cup milk
1 teaspoon ammonium carbonate (buy at drugstore)

Bring water and butter to a good boil. Add the flour while boiling and stir well until mass is thoroughly incorporated—about five minutes. • Remove from fire and allow to cool for ten minutes. Add eggs gradually. Then add the ammonium carbonate and last the milk, a little at a time. • Drop by teaspoonfuls on pans that are slightly greased. Bake at 450 degrees until browned.

TUNA STUFFING:

2 6½-ounce cans tuna, drained and flaked
⅔ cup celery, finely chopped
½ cup mayonnaise

4 tablespoons well-drained pickle relish
½ teaspoon salt
dash of pepper

Combine all ingredients; toss lightly to mix well. • Slit cooled shells and fill just before serving. Number of puffs depends on size of puff shells.

My constant prayers for you are a real joy, for they bring back to my mind how we have worked together for the gospel from the earliest days until now (Philippians 1:4–5, Phillips).

BANKERS' OATMEAL COOKIES

1 cup butter
1 cup brown sugar, packed
1 cup granulated sugar
2 eggs, well beaten
1 teaspoon vanilla extract
3 cups quick rolled oats

1½ cups sifted flour
1 teaspoon soda
1 teaspoon salt
1 3½-ounce can angel flake
   coconut

Cream together butter, brown sugar, granulated sugar. Add eggs, vanilla, and oats, blending thoroughly. Sift together flour, soda, and salt; add to egg-sugar mixture. Stir in coconut. • Roll dough into cylinders 1½ inches in diameter. Chill at least 2 hours. Slice ¼ inch thick and place on greased baking sheet. • Bake at 350 degrees for 10 minutes or until brown.

I thank my God for you Christians . . . whenever I think of you (Philippians 1:3, Phillips).

PASTORS' PUNCH   *About 35 punch cups*

2 cups orange juice
½ cup lemon juice

1½ quarts pineapple juice
4 1-quart bottles ginger ale

Combine first 3 ingredients; mix well. Pour over ice into large punch bowl. Fill bowl with ginger ale beverage.

Physical nourishment aids spiritual refreshment when
men gather for fellowship (baked spareribs—recipe, page 67)

MEN'S FELLOWSHIP

Let us have real warm affection for one another as between brothers, and a willingness to let the other man have the credit (Romans 12:10, Phillips).

The Men's Fellowship serves as a refreshing and spiritually nourishing time for the man in your house. If there are times when you wish you could have his companionship instead of having him give it to men in the church, just remember he should come home a better husband. Even though the official-dom of the church has long been a man's world, it is the women who provide the food, and in a real way are a part of Men's Fellowship.

Hot spiced cider smells good when the men come in, and it is a hearty man's drink. Heat cider with a few cloves and cinnamon sticks. Most men really enjoy it.

*Sesame Chicken or *Baked Spareribs
Tossed Salad with *Mustard Dressing   Assorted Relishes
French Rolls
*Wanda's Coconut Delight
or
*Peach Melba

Coffee   *Orange Iced Tea

Be sure to have lots of French rolls served in large baskets with checkered napkins.

SESAME CHICKEN   *4 to 6 servings*

2 broiler-fryer chickens,
   quartered
½ cup sesame seed
⅓ cup corn oil
4 tablespoons onion, minced
1 clove garlic, minced

2 teaspoons salt
½ teaspoon cardamom
½ teaspoon ginger
dash cloves
dash chili powder

Dip chicken in oil and then in sesame seed. Place chicken skin side down in shallow buttered baking dish. • Combine remaining ingredients; sprinkle chicken with mixture. • Bake chicken in 350 degree oven for 30 minutes. • Turn skin side up; continue baking until chicken is tender, about 30 minutes longer. Serve with sesame sauce if desired.

SAUCE:

Remove chicken pieces from baking dish. Blend 1 tablespoon corn starch with 1 cup water; stir into pan gravy. Cook over low heat, stirring constantly, until sauce thickens. Serve with chicken.

You can create some of your greatest successes by developing a palate for seasonings. Experiment with herbs, spices, condiments, fruit juices, vinegars, and flavoring extracts for your own specialties.

MUSTARD DRESSING   *About 2 cups*

1 cup mayonnaise
3 tablespoons prepared mustard
½ cup salad oil

½ cup cider vinegar
½ clove garlic, minced
salt and pepper

Mix all ingredients in a bowl. Season with salt and pepper to taste. Use with combination salad.

BAKED SPARERIBS   *12 servings*

8 pounds spareribs
salt
coarsely ground black pepper
¾ cup catsup
¼ cup tomato paste
4 tablespoons brown sugar
1 tablespoon light prepared
   mustard

2 tablespoons cider vinegar
4 to 5 drops liquid smoke
⅛ teaspoon ginger
⅛ teaspoon garlic powder
⅛ teaspoon onion powder
1 tablespoon soy sauce
4 cloves crushed garlic

Cut ribs into uniform individual servings—6 to 8 ribs per serving. Lay ribs in shallow pan, sprinkle with salt and coarsely ground black pepper and cover with cold water. • Cover and bake at 325 degrees for 1½ hours or until meat is tender. • While meat is baking, combine rest of ingredients in saucepan and bring to a boil. Season to taste with salt and pepper. • Remove spareribs from pan. Arrange servings, convex side of ribs up, in flat pan or container, lined with foil, and brush spareribs over entire surface with sparerib sauce. Bake in 325 degree oven until glaze has dried. • Turn meat and repeat the process. • Turn once more and apply a second layer of sauce to the convex side of the ribs. About 20 minutes will be required for each glazing. Use pastry brush to apply the sauce.

We repeat, we really saw and heard what we are now writing to you about. We want you to be with us in this—in this fellowship with the Father, and Jesus Christ his Son (1 John 1:3, Phillips).

WANDA'S COCONUT DELIGHT   *8 servings*

GRAHAM CRACKER CRUST:

1⅔ cups graham cracker
   crumbs

6 tablespoons melted butter
2 tablespoons sugar

Combine ingredients and press into 9 or 10-inch greased pie pan or cheesecake mold and bake 8 minutes at 350 degrees.

FILLING:

6 egg yolks
1 13-ounce can evaporated milk
2 cups granulated sugar
½ cup cornstarch

1½ cups shredded coconut
½ cup pecans, chopped
1 stick butter

Whip egg yolks with wire whip until mixed; add milk and the sugar combined with the cornstarch. Start cooking this mixture in *top* of double boiler. • While it is cooking, gradually add the coconut, pecans, and butter. Simmer until thickened and cornstarch is cooked. *Stir constantly.* Pour into shell. Cool.

TOPPING:

Whip 2 cups of chocolate dessert topping (according to directions on package) and spread on top of dessert. Chill until cold and set.

PEACH MELBA   *8 servings*

1 package frozen raspberries, puréed

2 17-ounce cans peach halves

1 pint vanilla ice cream or 1 package vanilla pudding (made according to directions)

If most husbands are like mine, they want something crunchy with soft desserts. Vanilla wafers or other crunchy cookies go well with peach Melba.

For raspberry purée, place one package of partially thawed raspberries in blender; beat at high speed for one minute. • Place a peach half in each of 8 sherbet glasses. Spoon 1 tablespoon of vanilla ice cream or vanilla pudding in center of each peach. Pour 2 tablespoons raspberry purée over the peach. Serve immediately.

ORANGE ICED TEA   *Serves 100*

4½ cups loose black tea

1 gallon boiling water

5½ gallons cold water

13 lemons

20 oranges

4 cups sugar

2 cups brown sugar

Place tea in a cloth bag large enough to hold at least 3 times this amount of tea; tie top with cord long enough for easy removal. Pour boiling water over the bag. • Cover, steep for 5 minutes; uncover and remove bag. • Add tea concentrate to cold water. Add juice of lemons and oranges and both sugars. Pour over cracked ice in tall glasses.

Baked in attractive casseroles, Mrs. Hatfield's sesame chicken
can go straight from the oven to the table (recipe, page 66)

MIDWEEK COMMITTEE
OR BOARD SESSION

Men have different gifts, but it is the same Spirit who gives them. There are different ways of serving God, but it is the same Lord who is served. God works through different men in different ways, but it is the same God who achieves his purposes through them all. Each man is given his gift by the Spirit that he may use it for the common good (1 Corinthians 12:4–7, Phillips).

We have come to a point where a great deal of our church business is handled by specialized committees. In order that the burden of church business be shared by many, these committee assignments should be rotated on an annual or biannual basis. If this is your year for the business of the church, I hope the following menu and recipes will be beneficial to you.

After the guests arrive, relax and enjoy yourself, while you are keeping an eye on what is going on. Try to serve the meal on time. If crises arise, take them in stride. Above all, plan so you can enjoy your guests and so they enjoy your fellowship.

Sweet and Sour Pork Chops
String Beans with Water Chestnuts
*Wedge of Lettuce Salad with *Dressing*
**Mrs. M.'s Pumpkin Loaf Cake with Whipped Cream*
Rolls   Coffee   Tea

MRS. ISAAK'S SWEET AND SOUR PORK CHOPS
12 servings

5 to 6 pounds of pork chops
½ cup flour
salt and pepper
2 cups onions, cut in rings
2 cups celery, cut
2 cups green peppers, sliced
½ cup catsup

2 tablespoons sweet pickle
  juice
2 tablespoons soy sauce
2 tablespoons Worcestershire
  sauce
¾ cup granulated sugar
¾ cup water

Trim fat from pork chops; then roll chops in flour, salt, and pepper. Place in 3-quart baking dish and cover with the vegetables. • Mix catsup, pickle juice, soy sauce, Worcestershire sauce, sugar, and water and pour over chops and vegetables. • Bake in 300 degree oven for 3 hours covered; uncover and bake ½ hour more.

STRING BEANS WITH WATER CHESTNUTS
12 servings

3 10-ounce packages string beans, frozen
1 6-ounce can water chestnuts, drained
salt and pepper

Cook 3 packages frozen string beans according to directions on package. Add water chestnuts which have been thinly sliced. Salt and pepper to taste.

THE OLD MULTNOMAH HOTEL'S SALAD DRESSING
1½ quarts

1 quart salad oil
1 cup wine vinegar
2 tablespoons lemon juice

2 tablespoons sugar
1 tablespoon paprika
salt and pepper to taste

Combine all ingredients in a bowl and beat with an electric mixer. This dressing is especially good over limestone or Bibb lettuce.

MRS. M.'S PUMPKIN LOAF CAKE   2 loaves

1 cup shortening
4 cups granulated sugar
6 eggs
1 No. 2 can pumpkin
5 cups sifted flour
3 teaspoons soda

1¼ teaspoons baking powder
2½ teaspoons salt
1½ teaspoons cinnamon
1½ teaspoons nutmeg
1 cup water
1½ teaspoons vanilla extract
nuts (optional)

"The glory of the house is hospitality" were the words of an early American fireplace motto. The pride and pleasure of entertaining in the home is one of our greatest joys.

Preheat oven to 350 degrees and grease two 9¾ x 5¾ x 2¾-inch loaf pans. • Cream shortening and sugar, using electric mixer. Add eggs one at a time and continue beating. • Add pumpkin and mix. • Sift flour, soda, baking powder, salt, cinnamon, and nutmeg together and add to the first mixture. Add water and vanilla; mix well. You may add a few chopped nuts. Pour into prepared pans and bake for about 45 minutes. • Cool for 5 minutes; then turn onto cooling rack. Serve slices with whipped cream if desired.

Garnishes give lamb curry with steamed rice an exotic look
to go with its Eastern flavor (recipe, page 76)

FAREWELL TO
THE DEPARTING MINISTER

After this the Lord appointed a further seventy-two and sent them on ahead in pairs to every town and place he was going to visit himself. He said to them: "The crop is heavy, but labourers are scarce; you must therefore beg the owner to send labourers to harvest his crop. Be on your way (Luke 10:1–3, NEB).

Whatever the reason for "Farewell to the Departing Minister," dinner in his honor should be given in a spirit of love and good fellowship. It is the time that you can express your gratitude for his efforts to be your spiritual leader, teacher, and friend. An appropriate gift to fit into the life-style of his next assignment should be provided. How about singing "Blessed be the tie that binds our hearts in Christian love" . . . with hands joined . . . to let him know that wherever he goes, he is a part of your fellowship circle?

Apricot Nectar
*Lamb Curry and Steamed Rice
Spiced Peach with Chutney
*Green Beans with Poppy Seed Dressing
Biscuits   Tea   Coffee
"Farewell" Sheetcake or *Lemon Pudding Cake

Apricot nectar will look prettier if it has a thin slice of lime on the top of it. Use your colorful assorted paper cups.

LAMB CURRY AND STEAMED RICE
8 generous servings

Appropriate curry garnishes are crumbled crisp bacon, chopped peanuts, crushed toasted almonds, raisins, chutney, and coconut.

Another attractive way to serve the lamb curry is to mound it in the center of a very deep-welled platter surrounded by a ring of steamed rice. Garnish with well-drained, crushed pineapple and sliced young green onion tops. The lamb curry can be stretched by adding a little more soup if you find you are having more people.

3 pounds boneless leg of lamb, cut into one-inch pieces
1 cup yogurt
2½ teaspoons salt
1 teaspoon ground cumin
1½ teaspoons ground turmeric
½ teaspoon ground cardamom
¼ cup salad oil
1½ cups chopped onion
1 clove garlic, crushed
1 teaspoon dried mustard
1 teaspoon ground ginger

½ teaspoon ground cinnamon
½ teaspoon freshly ground black pepper
¼ to ½ teaspoon cayenne pepper
⅛ teaspoon ground cloves
1 cup water
1 teaspoon lemon juice
2 tablespoons freshly grated coconut, or 2 tablespoons flaked coconut

In a mixing bowl, combine meat, yogurt, salt, cumin, turmeric, and cardamom; marinate two hours. • Heat one tablespoon oil in a skillet and brown meat. Pour off excess fat. • In another skillet, cook onion and garlic in remaining oil until golden. Add spices and cook, stirring, two minutes. Add lamb, cover and cook 20 minutes over medium heat. Add one cup water and mix. • Cover and simmer 30 minutes, adding more water only to keep from burning. • Just before serving, add lemon juice and coconut. Serve with plain rice and extra coconut.

POPPY SEED DRESSING   *About 4 cups*

1½ cups granulated sugar
2 teaspoons dry mustard
2 teaspoons salt
⅔ cup cider vinegar

3 tablespoons onion juice
2 cups salad oil
3 tablespoons poppy seed

Mix dry ingredients. Add vinegar and onion juice, mixing continually. Add salad oil and poppy seed. Store in cool place.

GREEN BEANS WITH POPPY SEED DRESSING

Use canned, cut green beans. Marinate for short period of time in Poppy Seed Dressing and chill. • Drain before serving. Garnish with chopped celery sprinkled over the top.

LEMON PUDDING CAKE   20 *servings*

1 cup (2 sticks) butter
2 cups granulated sugar
6 large eggs
3 cups cake flour
4 teaspoons baking powder
pinch of salt

1 cup milk
1 teaspoon lemon extract
1 teaspoon vanilla extract
1 4-ounce box lemon pie filling
1 pint cream, whipped
1 cup grated coconut

Cream butter; add sugar gradually and beat until light and fluffy. Add eggs one at a time, beating well after each addition. • Sift dry ingredients together and add to the butter mixture alternately with the milk, stirring after each addition. Add and stir in flavoring; pour into buttered 10 x 15-inch pan. • Bake in preheated oven at 350 degrees for 30 minutes or until done. Remove from pan and cool. • Prepare a 4-ounce box of lemon pie filling, following directions on box. Frost the cooled cake with the pie filling. • When frosting is set, spread with whipped cream and sprinkle with coconut. Chill.

Sprigs of mint and slices of citrus decorate Rock Cornish
game hens on serving platter (recipe, page 80)

THE FATHER–SON BANQUET

Children's children are the crown of old men; and the glory
of children are their fathers (Proverbs 17:6).

Man to man—that wonderful relationship between father and
son! The Father-Son Banquet is just one way that the church
community provides for a needed kind of fellowship. Today this
is particularly true when the father has, of necessity, to be away
from home much of the time or when the family is separated.
Young boys do need that male image . . . do need to identify
with their fathers or with male members of their families.

Most men like some-
thing to nibble on
when they arrive.
Serve an assortment
of nuts, chips, or raw
vegetable sticks
along with the juice.

Tomato or Cranberry Juice
*Rock Cornish Game Hen and Pilaf or
*French Ham and Cheese Fondue
Green Peas
Assorted Relish Tray
Rolls
*Chocolate Fudge Pie
Tea   Coffee

ROCK CORNISH GAME HEN   *8 servings*

Rock Cornish game hens are a pleasure to serve because they are unusual. Many excellent stuffings and sauces may be served with them, and they blend well with fruit and sweet-sour flavorings.

8 Rock Cornish game hens
2 whole bell peppers
4 ribs celery

2 medium small onions
1 clove garlic
1 tablespoon salt

Chop pepper, celery, and onion. Mix with one clove crushed garlic and 1 tablespoon salt. Stuff each hen with above filling. Place in greased glass baking dish, allowing about 2 inches between each bird. • Roast at 350 degrees for ½ hour; in meantime make:

SAUCE:

½ cup (1 stick) butter
1 cup honey
2 teaspoons grated orange peel
1 cup orange juice

3 11-ounce cans mandarin oranges, drained
4 teaspoons finely chopped mint (optional)

Melt butter. Combine all ingredients and heat until boiling. Pour over the browned birds and baste every 15 minutes, cooking them for 30 minutes longer. Serve with favorite pilaf recipe.

FRENCH HAM AND CHEESE FONDUE
8 servings

Chicken or seafood may be substituted for the ham in the fondue. Asparagus cut in 1-inch lengths may be used in place of ham for other occasions.

3 cups French bread
3 cups cooked ham
½ pound cheddar cheese
3 tablespoons flour

1 tablespoon dry mustard
3 tablespoons melted butter
4 eggs
2 cups milk

Cube the ham, bread, and cheese. Make a layer of one-third of the bread, ham, and cheese in a buttered 2-quart casserole. • Mix flour and mustard in a cup, sprinkle about 1 tablespoon over layer, drizzle 1 tablespoon butter over that. • Repeat with two more layers. • Beat eggs and milk until light in color and pour over bread mixture. Cover and chill in refrigerator overnight. • Bake uncovered in 350 degree oven for 1 hour. Serve at once.

CHOCOLATE FUDGE PIE   *8 servings*

NUT CRUST:

¼ cup soft margarine
¼ cup sugar

1 tablespoon all-purpose flour
1 cup finely chopped walnuts

Blend margarine with sugar, flour, and nuts. Press over bottom and sides (but not rim) of 9-inch pie plate.

FUDGE FILLING:

½ cup soft margarine
1 cup granulated sugar
3 eggs
2 envelopes unsweetened
  (no-melt) chocolate

⅓ cup sifted all-purpose flour
1 teaspoon vanilla extract
½ teaspoon baking powder
⅛ teaspoon salt

Place all ingredients in bowl; mix by hand with spoon until smooth. Turn into nut crust. • Bake in slow 325 degree oven 35 to 45 minutes. (Filling is slightly moist when done.) Serve warm or cool with vanilla ice cream or whipped cream.

HEARTS AND FLOWERS

Now that you have, by obeying the truth, made your souls clean enough for a genuine love of your fellows, see that you do love each other, fervently and from the heart (1 Peter 1:22, Phillips).

Doing a special thing in conjunction with an important occasion for a member of your church community or a staff member of your church should not be overlooked. Memorable occasions, given by you, such as bridal showers, rehearsal dinners, baby showers, and anniversary celebrations can be gifts of love never to be forgotten. Sometimes a couple finds that, due to family circumstances, widowed or deceased parents, they must make all the arrangements for the wedding. What greater way to express Christian love and fellowship than for someone in your Christian community to plan and host the rehearsal dinner or even the reception. A wedding is a Christian community event; Christ blessed it, "What therefore God has joined together, let no man put asunder" (Matthew 19:6, RSV).

A large pot of flowers on the front step is a very inviting way to say welcome to a party. Try one outside your door, or in the entry hall, next time you entertain.

. . . and all other commandments are summed up in this one saying: "Thou shalt love thy neighbor as thyself." Love hurts nobody: therefore love is the answer to the Law's commands (Romans 13:9–10, Phillips).

Wedding rehearsal dinner—memorable food for a memorable occasion (menu and recipes, pages 85 and 86)

Mirror reflects enticing invitation to taste spicy
spicy shrimp with steamed rice (recipe, page 85)

WEDDING REHEARSAL DINNER

Spicy Shrimp with Steamed Rice
Assorted Relishes
Rolls   Coffee   Tea
Assorted Cheeses and Crackers
Bride's Dessert

Cheeses should always be served at a temperature of about 70 degrees. Try mixing mild cheeses with the more ripened, aromatic or smoked ones. Garnish Brie cheese with fresh strawberries as pictured in the illustration on page 107.

SPICY SHRIMP   *8 servings*

3 pounds frozen shrimp,
  peeled and deveined
1 cup finely chopped onion
½ cup finely chopped scallions
2 to 4 garlic cloves, crushed
1½ cups butter or margarine
3 tablespoons cornstarch
2½ cups water
2 8-ounce cans tomato sauce

2 bay leaves
1 tablespoon Worcestershire
  sauce
¼ teaspoon hot pepper sauce
1 teaspoon salt
1 teaspoon sugar
1 lemon for garnish, sliced
5 cups cooked rice
parsley

Cook shrimp according to directions on package. • Cook onion, scallions, and garlic in butter until soft. Blend in cornstarch. Add water, tomato sauce, and all ingredients except shrimp and rice. Cover; simmer about 10 minutes, stirring occasionally. • Uncover, and continue cooking over low heat until mixture is reduced by about half. • Add shrimp and heat. Serve on fluffy rice garnished with parsley and lemon slices.

BRIDE'S DESSERT   *10 to 12 servings*

1 envelope gelatin
½ cup cold water
½ cup hot water
2 teaspoons vanilla extract

6 egg whites, room temperature
⅓ cup granulated sugar
1 pint whipping cream
1 package vanilla wafers (small)

Soak gelatin in cold water; then add to hot water; add the vanilla. • Beat egg whites until soft moist peaks form when beater is withdrawn. Add the sugar, about 2 tablespoons at a time, beating it in after each addition. Fold this mixture into the gelatin-vanilla mixture. • Whip cream and fold into the above. • Crush cookies, place half of these crumbs in buttered 9 x 15-inch pan and press them firmly. Spread mixture in pan and top with remaining crumbs. Press lightly again. Refrigerate 24 hours.

> Behold, you are beautiful, my beloved,
> truly lovely.
>
> As a lily among brambles,
> so is my love among maidens.
>
> As an apple tree among the trees of the wood,
> so is my beloved among young men.
> With great delight I sat in his shadow,
> and his fruit was sweet to my taste.
> He brought me to the banqueting house,
> and his banner over me was love.
>
> Many waters cannot quench love,
> neither can floods drown it.
> (Song of Solomon 1:16; 2:2–4; 8:7, NEB)

WEDDING RECEPTION

Bakery Bride's Cake
Assorted Tea Sandwiches
*Rolled Chicken Sandwiches
*Asparagus Roll Sandwiches
Nuts   Mints
*Wedding Ring Punch
Coffee   Tea

ROLLED CHICKEN SANDWICHES
24 sandwiches

1 loaf sandwich bread, white unsliced	1 cup evaporated milk
2 eggs, beaten	½ teaspoon Worcestershire sauce
1 tablespoon flour	1½ cups chopped, cooked chicken
¼ teaspoon salt	

Combine eggs, flour, salt, milk, Worcestershire sauce, and cook over hot water until thick; fold in chopped chicken. • Using a sharp knife, remove the crusts from the bread. Cut the bread, horizontally, into 5 very thin slices. Roll with rolling pin. Spread with filling and roll lengthwise. • Wrap in aluminum foil or plastic wrap and chill for several hours or overnight. • Cut into 1½-inch slices; place rolled edge down on lightly buttered baking sheets. • Before serving, put under broiler for a few minutes. *Watch carefully.* Serve immediately.

A variety of sandwich cutters is a great asset, as sandwiches cut in fancy shapes add to any occasion. Cut bread slices ahead of time; store, covered with barely dampened paper towels, in closed container in the refrigerator until ready to spread.

ASPARAGUS ROLL SANDWICHES
12 sandwiches

12 thin slices white bread
8 slices bacon, cooked,
   drained, and crumbled

2 3-ounce packages cream
   cheese, softened
12 cooked asparagus spears
melted butter

Trim crust from bread slices and roll with rolling pin to flatten slightly. Blend bacon bits with cream cheese and spread mixture on bread slices. Lay a cold, cooked asparagus spear on each slice of bread and roll up. Place on baking sheet, seam side down; cover and refrigerate until serving time. Then brush with melted butter and toast in broiler until lightly browned. Serve hot.

WEDDING RING PUNCH

Other decorative ice rings can be made by arranging orange, lemon, and lime slices, mint sprigs, grape clusters, strawberries, or cherries in the mold. Fill mold one-third full of water, add fruit, and freeze. When solid, fill mold with cold water and freeze.

2 22-ounce cans orange juice
   (canned, not frozen)
1 22-ounce can pineapple juice
1 8-ounce bottle pure lemon
   juice

1 32-ounce bottle cranberry
   juice
3 quarts of dry ginger ale
small amount of sugar to taste

The day before, make an ice ring by boiling 2 quarts of water and pouring it into a 2-quart ring mold and then freezing it immediately. Dip ice ring in hot water to unmold; place in bowl before pouring in punch. For a large punch bowl, add all the ingredients; sweeten to taste. For a smaller bowl, use half the amount listed above.

BRIDAL SHOWER MENU

Uncle Chuck's Macaroon Pudding
Wedding Veil Ice Cream Molds
Coffee   Tea
Mints   Nuts

UNCLE CHUCK'S MACAROON PUDDING
6 to 8 servings

1 pint whole milk
3 eggs, separated
¼ cup granulated sugar

1 tablespoon gelatin
2 tablespoons cold water
½ teaspoon vanilla extract
12 macaroons

Heat milk in top of double boiler. • Beat egg yolks and sugar together. Add the milk, stirring with a wire whisk. Return to the double boiler and cook until mixture coats spoon. • Remove from heat and mix in the gelatin which has been dissolved in cold water. Pour resulting custard over stiffly beaten egg whites and fold together gently. • Pour over a dozen or so macaroons which have been arranged in the bottom and on the sides of a 2-quart casserole. • Chill overnight.

WEDDING VEIL ICE CREAM MOLDS

Freeze 1 scoop of ice cream for each person. Cover these with whipped cream, beaten very stiff and slightly sweetened. Refreeze scoops. • Bend a short white pipe cleaner to form head and sew a small piece of white netting to top to form bridal veil. Place a veil on each scoop and put in white fluted baking cups; refreeze until ready to serve. Serve in the fluted cups.

A simple bakery bride's cake becomes a thing
of beauty when the hostess adds her own
decorative touches

FAMILY NIGHT SUPPER

Blessed is every one that feareth the Lord; that walketh in his ways. For thou shalt eat the labour of thine hands: happy shalt thou be, and it shall be well with thee. Thy wife shall be as a fruitful vine by the sides of thine house: thy children like olive plants round about thy table. Behold, that thus shall the man be blessed that feareth the Lord (Psalm 128:1-4).

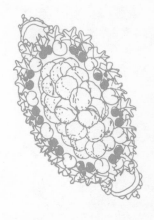

Lack of identity, particularly in urban centers, has been given by some as a reason for juvenile delinquency and the generation gap. The need to "belong" to a family, a church, a community is strong within us. Without this there is no tie, no feeling of togetherness, no reason to follow the prescribed path of righteousness. Why not plan a monthly or quarterly family night supper at the church?

*Grace's Applesauce Meatballs
*Olivia's Scalloped Potatoes
*Marinated Cucumber Slices
Carrots
Crusty Rolls   Milk and Coffee
Ice Cream Sandwiches

*Chicken Ginger with Rice
*Mary Jane's Frozen
Pineapple Salad
Asparagus or Broccoli
Sesame Rolls Milk and Coffee
Chocolate Cake

If you prefer, serve scoops of lime sherbet or vanilla ice cream heaped in the center of a large platter. Around this put fresh black cherries, plums, and apricots. Tuck in ivy leaves under fruit. Pass the tray at dessert time.

91

GRACE'S APPLESAUCE MEATBALLS
8 to 10 servings

Consider serving the meatballs or chicken ginger (p. 94) family style in large casseroles that could be put on each individual table.

1 pound ground beef
½ pound ground veal
½ pound ground fresh pork
1 cup soft bread crumbs, firmly packed
1 cup canned applesauce
2 eggs, slightly beaten

1 medium onion, grated; or
  1 teaspoon onion flakes
½ teaspoon mace
¼ teaspoon allspice
2 teaspoons salt
3 tablespoons margarine

Two pounds meat loaf mixture may be substituted for the meat. Mix the above ingredients except the margarine; then chill. Shape into 1-inch balls; brown slowly in margarine. • Remove meatballs to buttered 3-quart casserole (one with cover). • Pour off fat from skillet; measure and return ¼ cup of fat to skillet. Blend in ¼ cup flour.

ADD:

1 10¾-ounce can condensed consommé
1 cup water

2 tablespoons chopped parsley
salt to taste

Cook the above ingredients, stirring constantly until mixture boils and thickens. Pour over meatballs in casserole; cover and cook in preheated 375 degree oven for 45 minutes. • These meatballs may be frozen and reheated before serving.

Except the Lord build the house, they labour in vain that build it: except the Lord keep the city, the watchman waketh in vain (Psalm 127:1).

OLIVIA'S SCALLOPED POTATOES
8 to 10 servings

10 medium potatoes   1 can consommé
2 cups boiling water

Boil unpeeled potatoes in 2 cups water and 1 can consommé.
Cook until tender but still firm. Drain. When cool, peel potatoes
and slice. Place in layers in buttered 2-quart casserole.

SAUCE:

1½ cups medium white sauce   crisp bacon, green onions,
1 pint sour cream   and/or cheddar cheese
salt and pepper

Combine white sauce and sour cream. Season to taste with salt
and pepper. Pour sauce over potatoes. Put crisp bacon, green
onions, and/or cheddar cheese over top. Bake about 30 minutes
at 350 degrees.

MARINATED CUCUMBER SLICES
4 to 6 servings

½ cup cider vinegar   dash of white pepper
¼ cup salad oil   1 teaspoon dill weed
¼ teaspoon salt   1 medium-sized cucumber

Blend first 5 ingredients in a bowl. Thinly slice cucumber; add to
marinade and mix lightly. Chill several hours or overnight.

CHICKEN GINGER *12 servings*

3 fryer chickens, cut into
  pieces
2 teaspoons seasoned salt

3 cans cream of chicken soup
1½ teaspoons ginger

Use 3-quart shallow baking dish. Sprinkle chicken pieces with seasoned salt. Pour undiluted cream of chicken soup to which ginger has been added over chicken. • Marinate at least 3 hours. • Bake uncovered at 325 degrees for 1½ hours. (Chicken can be marinated in the morning and then baked 1½ hours just before serving time.)

My children, let us love not merely in theory or in words— let us love in sincerity and in practice (1 John 3:18, Phillips).

MARY JANE'S FROZEN PINEAPPLE SALAD
10 servings

1 pint dairy sour cream
2 tablespoons lemon juice
¾ cup granulated sugar
⅛ teaspoon salt

1 9-ounce can crushed
  pineapple, drained
¼ cup chopped maraschino
  cherries
¼ cup chopped walnuts
1 banana, sliced

Mix sour cream, lemon juice, sugar, and salt. Add remaining ingredients and blend. Pour into medium muffin tins which have been lined with paper baking cups. Freeze until firm. Remove papers to serve. Mixture will fill 10 cups.

SATURDAY NIGHT YOUTH
FELLOWSHIP

Let no one slight you because you are young, but make yourself an example to believers in speech and behaviour, in love, fidelity, and purity (1 Timothy 4:12, NEB).

Mothers of very young children are accustomed to hearing "What can I do?" This question seems to be even stronger as children grow into young adulthood. Even though they have a growing feeling of independence, they are sometimes at a loss to provide wholesome and worthwhile recreation for themselves. A strong youth program in a church is worth whatever price it costs in terms of time, personnel, and money. Youth do need more direction than they are willing to admit they need or more than some sociologists are willing to grant them.

*Saturday Night Youth Punch
*Frilly Drumsticks
*Potato Salad
*Coconut Orange Mold Salad
*Brownie Drops
*Pecan Balls
Ice Cream with *Mary B.'s Chocolate Sauce

The drumstick has traditionally been the favorite part of the chicken for young people. It is less costly, too.

95

SATURDAY NIGHT YOUTH PUNCH

Kool-Aid   ginger ale beverage

Mix together equal parts of Kool-Aid and ginger ale in large punch bowl.

To make paper frills for the drumsticks, use 8½ x 11-inch white or colored paper. Fold sheet in half crosswise, then fold again crosswise. With a pair of scissors cut the fold at ¼-inch intervals to within ¾ inch of the open edge. Unfold the second fold and cut sheet of paper in half. Then reverse the paper and bring the edges together again. This gives the frill a puffed effect.

To place on drumstick, roll the uncut portion of the paper to fit the end of the drumstick, cut, and secure with cellophane tape. One sheet of paper should make 6 frills.

FRILLY DRUMSTICKS

2 drumsticks per person   salad oil
cornflakes

Coat each drumstick with oil and roll in crushed cornflakes. Bake at 350 degrees for 40 minutes, or until brown and done.

POTATO SALAD   *8 servings*

½ cup mayonnaise   ½ teaspoon pepper
½ cup sour cream   ½ teaspoon dill seed
2 tablespoons white vinegar   4 cups diced, cooked potatoes
1 tablespoon prepared mustard   ½ small cucumber, peeled,
2 teaspoons granulated sugar   seeded and chopped
1½ teaspoons salt   2 green onions, chopped

In large bowl, blend mayonnaise, sour cream, vinegar, mustard, sugar, salt, pepper and dill seed. Add remaining ingredients; toss gently until well mixed. • Refrigerate to develop flavors until serving time. Serve on crisp greens, if you like.

COCONUT ORANGE MOLD SALAD
10 to 12 servings

2 3-ounce packages orange
  gelatin
1½ cups hot water
2¼ cups juices, canned
  orange and pineapple

1 medium can crushed
  pineapple, drained
½ pint sour cream
½ 3½-ounce can coconut
1 can mandarin oranges

Mix gelatin with hot water and orange and pineapple juices. Chill until slightly thickened. Add crushed pineapple, sour cream, and coconut. Place in 2-quart mold. Chill. • Garnish with mandarin oranges.

BROWNIE DROPS   *5 dozen*

2 4-ounce packages of German
  sweet chocolate
1 tablespoon butter or
  margarine
2 eggs
¾ cup granulated sugar

¼ cup unsifted flour
¼ teaspoon baking powder
¼ teaspoon cinnamon
⅛ teaspoon salt
½ teaspoon vanilla extract
¾ cup pecans, finely chopped

Melt chocolate and butter over hot water. Cool. • Beat eggs until foamy. Then add sugar, 2 tablespoons at a time, and beat until thickened (about 5 minutes by an electric mixer). Blend in chocolate; add dry ingredients, vanilla, and nuts. Chill. • Drop from a teaspoon onto greased baking sheets. Bake at 350 degrees for 8 to 10 minutes until cookies feel "set" when lightly touched. Do not overbake.

PECAN BALLS   *5 dozen*

1 cup butter or margarine
½ cup granulated sugar
½ teaspoon salt
2 cups sifted flour

1 teaspoon almond extract
2 cups pecans, finely chopped
confectioners' sugar

Cream together butter and sugar; add salt, flour, almond extract and pecans. Mix well. Chill dough for several hours. Form into walnut-sized balls. Place on ungreased cookie sheets. Bake in 350 degree oven, 12 to 15 minutes. Transfer to wire racks. While still warm, roll in confectioners' sugar. When cookies have cooled completely, sprinkle with more confectioners' sugar.

And if it seem evil unto you to serve the Lord, choose you this day whom ye will serve; whether the gods which your fathers served that were on the other side of the flood, or the gods of the Amorites, in whose land ye dwell; but as for me and my house, we will serve the Lord (Joshua 24:15).

MARY B.'S CHOCOLATE SAUCE

1 cup granulated sugar
dash of salt
2½ tablespoons cornstarch

½ 13-ounce can evaporated
  milk
1 16-ounce can chocolate syrup

In top of double boiler, mix sugar, salt, and cornstarch together; gradually blend in milk and chocolate syrup. Cook over hot water until sauce is thickened.

NEW MEMBERS' DINNER

"Repent," said Peter, "repent and be baptized, every one of you, in the name of Jesus the Messiah for the forgiveness of your sins; and you will receive the gift of the Holy Spirit. For the promise is to you, and to your children, and to all who are far away, everyone whom the Lord our God may call" (Acts 2:38–39, NEB).

To keep from wondering, "Who's that sitting next to the Smiths?" you might plan a dinner for new members of the church to be given by the church. To offer the right hand of fellowship to newcomers is very important to them, and it could be the beginning of a friendship that is invaluable to you.

To make apple juice punch, combine equal amounts of chilled apple juice and ginger ale. Serve over cracked ice. Allow about 6 to 8 ounces per person.

*Apple Juice Punch

*Ann's Tamale Pie

*Cole Slaw

French Bread

Lemon Sherbet

Assorted Cookies

Coffee   Tea

To prepare sherbet ahead, use colorful 5-ounce paper cups. You and your committee can dish these out ahead of time and store them in the freezer.

ANN'S TAMALE PIE   *12 servings*

Your Committee of Seven can prepare the tamale pie. Why not rent colored tablecloths to add zest to the New Members' Dinner? Red, green, or blue would make a dramatic background. Or, you might prefer to use some of the very heavy paper table coverings convenient for church suppers or other large gatherings which are on the market now.

4 tablespoons olive oil
3 pounds ground beef, chuck
½ pound chorizo (Mexican sausage)
1 teaspoon garlic powder
1 large onion, chopped
2 1-pound cans tomatoes

2 8-ounce cans tomato sauce
2 16-ounce cans corn
2 4½-ounce cans chopped ripe olives
2 tablespoons chili powder
2 tablespoons salt

Brown beef and chorizo in oil. Add and stir in remaining ingredients. Pour into 3-quart casserole.

TOPPING:

2 eggs, beaten
1 cup milk

½ cup yellow corn meal
½ cup olive oil

Combine topping ingredients and pour over beef mixture. Bake at 350 degrees for 45 minutes to an hour.

COLE SLAW   *36 servings*

½ teaspoon salt
1½ cups granulated sugar
¼ teaspoon dry mustard

1 cup cider vinegar
3½ to 4 cups mayonnaise
cabbage, finely chopped

Dissolve salt, sugar, and mustard in vinegar. Add mayonnaise, stirring until smooth. Add this dressing in generous amounts to crisp, finely chopped cabbage until the slaw is liquid and creamy. • Marinate the slaw in the refrigerator for at least overnight. Five cups of dressing is adequate to 3 quarts of finely chopped cabbage. • Drain before serving.

SINGSPIRATION

O sing unto the Lord a new song:
    sing unto the Lord, all the earth.
Sing unto the Lord, bless his name;
    shew forth his salvation from day to day.
                    (Psalm 96:1–2)

Getting together on Sunday evening to "sing His praises" can be one of the most stimulating and enjoyable kinds of Christian fellowship. Even those who are monotones can enjoy the wonders of God's music. A perfect ending to a holy day—it will make Monday look brighter.

*Singspiration Punch or Hot Chocolate
*Ann's Orange Sponge Cake
Nuts

O come, let us sing unto the Lord: let us make a joyful noise to the rock of our salvation. Let us come before his presence with thanksgiving, and make a joyful noise unto him with psalms (Psalm 95:1–2).

I have one or two favorite arrangements of dried flowers that I like to use on my table in the fall. Another autumn favorite is bright red apples in a Paul Revere bowl, a simple but beautiful centerpiece. During the winter months, a fire in the fireplace is always inviting.

SINGSPIRATION PUNCH
12 to 18 servings

½ cup instant tea powder
2 quarts water
1 6-ounce can frozen limeade
1 6-ounce can frozen lemonade

1 6-ounce can frozen
  pineapple juice
1 22-ounce can canned orange
  juice

In large container, place instant tea; gradually add water, stirring until tea is dissolved. Add frozen juice concentrates; stir in orange juice. Chill thoroughly. Pour over ice ring in punch bowl to serve.

ANN'S ORANGE SPONGE CAKE
10-inch tube pan

4 eggs, separated
1 cup granulated sugar
juice of 1 orange

1 cup cake flour
1 teaspoon vanilla extract

Cream sugar and egg yolks until light and fluffy. Stir in orange juice and flour. Beat egg whites until stiff and fold into mixture. Pour into 10-inch tube pan. • Bake at 350 degrees for 30 minutes or until cake springs back to touch. Invert pan and cool. Remove from pan and glaze.

ORANGE GLAZE:

1 cup confectioners' sugar
2 tablespoons orange juice

1 tablespoon water

Combine confectioners' sugar with orange juice. Beat until smooth, adding up to 1 tablespoon water until the right consistency is reached.

AFTER CHOIR PRACTICE

It is a good thing to give thanks unto the Lord, and to sing praises unto thy name, O Most High: To show forth thy loving-kindness in the morning, and thy faithfulness every night, Upon an instrument of ten strings, and upon the psaltery; upon the harp with a solemn sound (Psalm 92: 1–3).

Food served late in the evening after choir practice should be filling and nourishing without being heavy. Soup seems to fit into this category. Pick and choose from among the following suggestions.

Melted Cheddar Cheese on English Muffin

Sesame French Bread

Chris's Soup Mix

Clam Chowder

French Onion Soup

Cheese Crisps

Olive Tarts

Orange Spice Cookies

Pearl's Chocolate Balls

After choir practice, have the group gather at your house for nourishing fare. This menu can be ready in minutes if the soup is prepared beforehand. Serve the soup in mugs. Arrange the other food on a buffet where guests can help themselves. Double or triple recipes as needed.

Melted cheddar cheese on English muffins is a great favorite. You can do many at one time by placing them on cookie sheets in the oven.

MELTED CHEDDAR CHEESE ON ENGLISH MUFFIN

½ English muffin per person

Sprinkle with 2 tablespoons grated cheddar cheese. Melt under broiler in oven on cookie sheet until cheese bubbles. Serve immediately.

SESAME FRENCH BREAD   *serves 18*

1 2½-ounce package sesame seeds
2 loaves French bread
butter

Sesame French bread goes well with various soups. The soups may be made ahead and reheated.

Sprinkle 1 2½-ounce package sesame seeds on a cookie sheet and toast in a moderate 350 degree oven for 5 minutes. Slice French bread ½ inch thick and brush one side of each slice with melted butter. Then place each slice on top of the toasted sesame seeds, buttered side down. Transfer bread, buttered side up, to another cookie sheet. Toast under broiler and serve immediately.

CLAM CHOWDER   *8 servings*

4 strips bacon, chopped
1 small onion, minced
2 stalks celery, chopped finely
2 potatoes, cooked, diced
½ teaspoon parsley flakes
½ teaspoon coarsely ground
  pepper

dash of garlic salt
1 to 2 cups minced clams
  (canned)
1½ quarts of milk
salt to taste
fresh parsley for garnish

Fry bacon until crisp; remove bacon and sauté one small minced onion in drippings. Then combine all ingredients in saucepan and heat to boiling. Do not let boil; serve immediately with fresh chopped parsley on top.

FRENCH ONION SOUP   *10 servings*

3 large onions, sliced
½ cup (1 stick) butter, browned
2 teaspoons flour
1½ cups tomato juice

4½ cups homemade beef stock (or 2 cans beef bouillon)
1 loaf of French bread
¾ cup Parmesan cheese, grated
salt to taste

For a large party, a chafing dish may double as a server–warmer for soup.

Sauté onions together in browned butter. Add flour, tomato juice, and stock. (If using canned bouillon, dilute 2 cans with water to make 4½ cups.) Simmer 4 hours and season. Serve with slice of toasted French bread which has been sprinkled with grated Parmesan cheese floating on top of soup.

CHRIS'S SOUP MIX

1 pound Canadian bacon
10 carrots
1 stalk of celery, leaves and all

6 large onions
2 cups parsley
4 tablespoons basil

Fry half the bacon; drain. Put it and all other ingredients together through meat grinder. Then simmer until done. Freeze in paper cups about ½ cup in size. To use, cook ½ cup with 2 cups tomato juice or water. What a great way to have the soup almost ready to go!

CHEESE CRISPS   *4 to 6 dozen*

2½ to 3 cups flour
½ teaspoon salt
½ teaspoon crushed red
  peppers

1 pound extra sharp cheddar
  cheese
1 cup (2 sticks) melted
  margarine

Combine flour, salt, and red pepper in large mixing bowl. Grate cheese and mix well with dry ingredients; stir in melted margarine. Knead to hold together. Roll ¼ inch thick on floured pastry board. Cut into 2 x ¼-inch strips. Place on baking sheet. Preheat oven to 300 degrees; put in oven and turn back to 250 degrees. Bake for 1 hour or until golden brown.

OLIVE TARTS   *4 dozen*

1 cup sifted flour
½ teaspoon salt
1 teaspoon paprika
2 cups grated sharp cheese

½ cup (1 stick) soft
  margarine
48 stuffed green olives
red pepper, if desired

Sift dry ingredients together. Blend in cheese and margarine and mix thoroughly. Wrap 1 teaspoon of mixture completely around each olive and arrange on cookie sheet and freeze. Remove from cookie sheet and store in plastic container in freezer. When desired, bake them 15 minutes at 400 degrees in preheated oven and serve warm. Allow 2 per person.

Buffet elegance with cheese, fruit, and flowers

ORANGE SPICE COOKIES *7 dozen*

Finger food in the form of orange spice cookies and chocolate balls seems to work better for after choir practice than a more formal kind of dessert.

1 cup (2 sticks) butter
1½ cups sugar
1 egg
2 tablespoons light corn syrup
3 cups sifted all-purpose flour

2 teaspoons soda
2 teaspoons cinnamon
2 teaspoons ginger
½ teaspoon cloves
1 tablespoon shredded orange peel

Cream butter and sugar. Add egg and syrup. Beat well. • Sift together dry ingredients. Mix into creamed mixture. • Add peel. • Shape into two 12-inch rolls, 2 inches in diameter. • Refrigerate for at least an hour. Slice ⅛ inch thick and place on greased cookie sheet about 1½ inches apart. • Bake 5 to 6 minutes at 400 degrees.

PEARL'S CHOCOLATE BALLS

2 cups walnuts, chopped
2 cups dates, chopped
2 cups crunchy peanut butter
2 cups confectioners' sugar

4 tablespoons melted butter (melt and measure)
1 12-ounce package chocolate chips
⅓ block paraffin

Chop walnuts and dates finely and mix well with peanut butter, sugar, and butter. Use hands. • Roll into balls about the size of a quarter or fifty-cent piece. Put on cookie sheet covered with waxed paper. • In top of double boiler melt chocolate chips and shave in paraffin while still in double boiler. Dip balls in chocolate with two teaspoons, placing ball between the spoons. • Let them stand on waxed paper until thoroughly cool and set. Store in tight container. Do not freeze.

AGAPE

Addressing his host, Jesus said: "When you give a luncheon
or a dinner party, don't invite your friends or your brothers
or relations or wealthy neighbors, for the chances are they
will invite you back, and you will be fully repaid. No, when
you give a party, invite the poor, the lame, the crippled, and
the blind. That way lies real happiness for you. They have
no means of repaying you, but you will be repaid when good
men are rewarded—at the resurrection."

Then, one of the guests, hearing these remarks of Jesus,
said,

"What happiness for a man to eat a meal in the kingdom
of God!" (Luke 14:12–15, Phillips).

A new missionary project, the "coffee house," has been added to
the "soup kitchen" to broaden the scope of the mission field to
the young up-and-outers and the disenchanted. Two such coffee
houses with which I am familiar are the Agape and the Potter's
House in Washington, D.C. Many others here as well as throughout the country are doing their part to bring the message of
Christ to those so desperately in need of hope and salvation. The
mainstay of both of the aforementioned operations is coffee,
served by people with loving and open hearts. "Love one another
as I have loved you." How easy it is to love the lovely, but what
about the unlovely who walk through the doors, hoping to find

Foods listed here are
intended to be eaten
as finger food. Keep
them available all
the time, along with
plenty of cold milk
and hot coffee. Use
red and white
checkered tablecloths
and red and white
plastic-coated paper
plates to create a
warm atmosphere.

In cooking spaghetti, always use a kettle large enough to hold, without boiling over, water 3 times the volume of the spaghetti. You may put a small amount of fat in the water to help keep the spaghetti from clumping and the water from boiling over. The spaghetti should be added to the water so gradually that the brisk boiling is not disturbed. Cook long spaghetti without breaking it. Hold it securely as you gradually submerge

it in the boiling water; as it softens, you will be able to push it completely into the boiling water. Do not over-cook. It should be

a friend, and who are delighted to find that friend in the person of Jesus? The agape or love feast, which is sometimes a feature of these coffee houses, may provide the first square meal some of their visitors have had in a long time. Spaghetti is always a favorite among young people. Combined with a large tossed salad and sourdough French bread, you have a meal. Choose snacks from the following recipes to have on hand with plenty of hot coffee.

Dida's Spaghetti

Wheat Nut Rolls

Date Nut Bread

Ella's Brownies (2)

Mrs. J.'s Orange Cake

Chocolate Pound Cake

Jan's Spiced Cider

DIDA'S SPAGHETTI   *8 servings*

2 tablespoons olive oil
2 pounds ground round steak
1 large onion, chopped
1 clove garlic, minced
1 stalk celery, chopped
1 6-ounce can tomato paste
1 cup beef stock or canned
  bouillon
1 to 2 cups water
1 teaspoon parsley

1 bay leaf
juice of 1 orange and peel
juice of ½ lemon and peel
2 tablespoons sugar
dash of nutmeg, cinnamon,
  and cloves
salt and pepper to taste
1 pound spaghetti
Parmesan cheese

Heat olive oil in large skillet. Stir in and sauté onion, garlic, celery, and ground steak. When the meat is nearly done, add the rest of the sauce ingredients. • Simmer 2 to 3 hours. Add water if necessary. • Remove orange and lemon peel and adjust seasoning. • Serve over spaghetti, cooked according to directions on package, with Parmesan cheese.

Share the happiness of those who are happy, and the sorrow of those who are sad (Romans 12:15, Phillips).

WHEAT NUT ROLLS

2 cups water	2 cups scalded milk
½ teaspoon salt	(cooled to warm)
1 cup bulghur	¼ cup shortening
1 cake yeast	1 egg
½ cup sugar	6 cups flour (3 cups at time)
1 teaspoon salt	

Bring to boil 2 cups water, ½ teaspoon salt; add 1 cup bulghur. Cover and simmer 20 minutes. • Combine in large bowl—1 cake yeast, ½ cup sugar, 1 teaspoon salt, 2 cups scalded milk, ¼ cup shortening, and 1 egg. Add 3 cups flour; beat 10 minutes in mixer. Add cooked bulghur; then add last 3 cups flour. Knead 8 to 10 minutes. • Let rise twice. • Shape into rolls and bake at 400 degrees for 20 minutes or use two loaf pans and bake at 450 degrees first 10 minutes, then 350 degrees for 25 minutes. • Cover bread with foil last 15 minutes.

tender but with a slight resilience or, as the Italians say, *al dente*. When the spaghetti is done, immediately add 1 cup of cold water to the kettle to stop the cooking without chilling the spaghetti. Immediately empty the spaghetti into a colander to drain. Have a hot platter ready with 2 to 4 tablespoons of butter on it. Add the spaghetti and toss. In Italy, spaghetti is served in one dish, the sauce in another, and grated cheese in a third.

Bulghur, used in the wheat nut rolls, is a parched cracked wheat. It can be bought at health food stores and specialty shops if your local supermarket does not stock it.

DATE NUT BREAD   *4 small loaves*

4 cups dates, cut up
2 cups nuts, chopped
2 cups boiling water
½ cup shortening
1½ cups brown sugar

2 eggs
4 cups sifted flour
1 teaspoon salt
2 teaspoons soda

Preheat oven to 350 degrees. Grease and flour 4 small loaf pans or 2 regular size loaf pans. • Let dates and nuts stand in boiling water. • Mix thoroughly the shortening, brown sugar, and eggs. Add date mixture. Sift flour before measuring and then sift together flour, salt, and soda into mixture and stir. Pour into prepared pans. • Bake for 45 to 50 minutes.

ELLA'S CHOCOLATE BROWNIES #1
16 squares

3 1-ounce squares unsweetened
  chocolate
½ cup (1 stick) margarine
2 eggs, beaten with 1 cup sugar
1 teaspoon vanilla extract

½ cup all-purpose flour
½ teaspoon baking powder
½ teaspoon salt
1 cup walnuts, coarsely
  chopped

Preheat oven to 350 degrees. Grease 8-inch square pan. • Melt chocolate and margarine in double boiler. Remove from heat and add eggs, beaten with sugar, and vanilla. Add sifted flour, baking powder, and salt. Stir in walnuts. • Bake in prepared pan for 25 minutes. Cool before cutting. Cut into 16 squares.

ELLA'S SAUCEPAN BROWNIES   *16 squares*

1/3 cup shortening
2 1-ounce squares unsweetened
  chocolate
1 cup granulated sugar
2 eggs

1/2 cup all-purpose flour
1/8 teaspoon salt
1/4 teaspoon baking powder
1 teaspoon vanilla extract
1/2 cup nuts, chopped

Preheat oven to 350 degrees. Grease an 8-inch square baking pan.
• Melt chocolate and shortening in saucepan over very low heat.
• Remove from heat and cool. Combine sugar with chocolate mixture; then beat in eggs, one at a time. Add and stir in dry ingredients, vanilla, and nuts. Spread in prepared pan and bake for 25 to 30 minutes. • Cut in squares or bars when cool.

MRS. J.'S ORANGE CAKE   *8 to 10 servings*

1 orange, juice and peel
1½ cups granulated sugar
1 cup raisins
½ cup shortening
2 eggs
1 cup sour milk

1 rounded teaspoon soda,
  dissolved in 1 tablespoon
  hot water
1 teaspoon vanilla extract
2 cups all-purpose flour

Preheat oven to 350 degrees. Grease and flour loaf pan. • Stir together orange juice and ½ cup sugar. Set aside. • Grind raisins and orange peel 3 times. • Cream shortening and 1 cup sugar; add eggs, one at a time, beating after each addition. Stir in milk and soda mixture. Add and stir in ground orange peel and raisins, vanilla, and flour. Bake in prepared pan for 45 minutes or until it tests done. • Pour juice and sugar mixture over hot cake. Let stand in pan. Serve plain or with whipped cream.

CHOCOLATE POUND CAKE
12 to 14 servings

1 cup (2 sticks) butter
  or margarine
2½ cups granulated sugar
6 eggs
3 cups sifted flour

½ teaspoon salt
½ teaspoon baking powder
½ cup cocoa
1 cup milk
1 teaspoon vanilla extract

Preheat oven to 325 degrees. Grease and flour 10-inch tube pan.
• Cream butter until light and fluffy. Add sugar gradually, creaming well. Beat in eggs, one at a time. Sift flour, measure, and then sift twice again with salt, baking powder, and cocoa. Mix dry ingredients into butter mixture, alternately with milk, beating just until blended. Stir in vanilla. Turn into pan. • Bake for 1 hour and 40 minutes or until a toothpick inserted comes out clean. Let cool on rack before removing from pan.

JAN'S SPICED CIDER
12 to 16 servings

2 quarts cider
¼ cup brown sugar, packed
1 teaspoon whole allspice

1 teaspoon whole cloves
2 cinnamon sticks
½ lemon, thinly sliced

Combine all ingredients in a 3-quart pan. Bring slowly to boiling point. Simmer 20 minutes. Strain and serve hot.

BIBLE STUDY GROUP

Try hard to show yourself worthy of God's approval, as a labourer who need not be ashamed, driving a straight furrow, in your proclamation of the truth (2 Timothy 2:15, NEB).

And how can you teach correctly if you have not studied? Can you keep in good physical condition by exercising once a year, in good health by eating once a week? How then can your soul be nourished if you only partake of the Word of God once a week? The Bible Study Group provides that additional nourishment for hungry souls who are searching and who can then teach others the Good News of salvation.

By simplifying your approach to entertaining, you'll find that hospitality need be neither hectic nor haphazard. Plan the event, organize your resources, and prepare as much of the food as possible beforehand. You will be calm and composed when your guests arrive.

MORNING
Papaya Juice
*Coffee Cake or
*Marie's Walnut Bars
Coffee   Tea

AFTERNOON
*Mrs. M.'s Summer Salad
*Mrs. Cooley's Butter Biscuits
Mints
Coffee   Tea

EVENING
*Split Pea Soup
Crackers
*Alicia's Apple Pudding
Coffee

The first soup mentioned in writing— the "mess of pottage" for which Esau sold his birthright to Jacob—was made with lentils.

COFFEE CAKE   *10 to 12 servings*

TOPPING:

¾ cup granulated sugar
1 cup brown sugar, packed
1 teaspoon cinnamon

3 graham cracker squares,
   rolled into fine crumbs
½ cup walnuts, chopped
¼ cup (½ stick) butter

Sift together white and brown sugar to make sugar mix. For topping, take only ¾ cup of the sugar mix, cinnamon, graham crackers, and butter and blend together until they crumble. Stir in nuts and set aside.

CAKE:

2½ cups all-purpose flour
1 cup of sugar mix, left
   from above sugar mix
1 teaspoon salt
1 teaspoon cinnamon

2 teaspoons baking powder
1 egg
¾ cup salad oil
1 cup milk

Preheat oven to 375 degrees. Lightly grease a 9 x 13-inch pan. • Mix together all of the cake ingredients and pour into prepared pan. Top with prepared topping and bake 30 to 35 minutes. Serve warm.

For the word of God is alive and active. It cuts more keenly than any two-edged sword, piercing as far as the place where life and spirit, joints and marrow, divide (Hebrews 4:12, NEB).

MARIE'S WALNUT BARS   *24 squares*

3 eggs	½ teaspoon baking soda
2 cups brown sugar, packed	pinch of salt
1 cup all-purpose flour	1½ cups walnuts, chopped

Preheat oven to 350 degrees. Grease a 9 x 13-inch pan. • Beat eggs well; add brown sugar and beat well. Sift together flour, baking soda, and salt. Combine with first mixture. Then add and stir in chopped walnuts; pour into prepared pan. • Bake about 20 minutes or until cake rebounds to the touch when pressed gently in the center. • Cool slightly and cut into 2-inch squares.

MRS. M.'S SUMMER SALAD
8 to 10 servings

1 cooked breast of turkey (approx. 4 to 5 cups)	1 to 1½ cups mayonnaise
	1 teaspoon curry powder
2 cups white seedless grapes, halved	salt and pepper to taste
	lettuce leaves
2 cups pineapple tidbits, drained	4 hard-boiled eggs
	parsley

Dice turkey; combine with grapes and pineapple tidbits. Toss lightly with mayonnaise which has been seasoned with the curry powder. Season to taste with salt, pepper. • Chill. • Pile ½-cup portions into crisp lettuce cups. Garnish with slices of hard-boiled eggs and sprigs of parsley.

MRS. COOLEY'S BUTTER BISCUITS
24 *small biscuits*

2 cups all-purpose flour	1 tablespoon sugar
4 teaspoons baking powder	1 cup (2 sticks) butter
½ teaspoon salt	¾ cup milk, approximately
½ teaspoon cream of tartar	

Preheat oven to 450 degrees. Grease baking sheet. • Sift the flour, baking powder, salt, cream of tartar, and sugar into a mixing bowl. With a pastry blender or 2 knives cut in butter until mixture has the texture of coarse corn meal. Stir gently with fork while adding milk. • Knead on lightly floured board for about 30 seconds. • Roll dough on floured board until it is ¾-inch thick. Cut with floured small biscuit cutter and place on baking sheet at 1-inch intervals. • Bake for 12 to 15 minutes or until golden brown. Serve immediately. These biscuits may be made ahead and then reheated before serving.

Thy word is a lamp unto my feet, and a light unto my path (Psalm 119:105).

SPLIT PEA SOUP   *8 to 10 servings*

In the evening, when many people have had their dinner but some have come from work and have not eaten, soup seems an appropriate choice to serve.

3 quarts water	1 quart half and half cream
1 ham bone	salt and pepper to taste
2 carrots, sliced	celery salt to taste
3 onions	curry powder to taste
3 sticks celery, sliced	Worcestershire sauce to taste
1 16-ounce package split peas	

Simmer ham bone; carrots; 2 of the onions, sliced; and celery in water for 6 hours. • Strain and put in refrigerator until fat solidifies on top. Remove fat. • Bring to a boil and add 1 chopped onion and split peas which have been washed. Cook until peas are soft, approximately 3 to 3½ hours, stirring occasionally as peas may stick to bottom of pot. • Put soup through a sieve. Add half and half cream. Season to taste with salt, pepper, celery salt, curry powder, and Worcestershire sauce. Reheat. • If soup is not thick enough, thicken with a little flour or corn starch mixed thoroughly with a small amount of water. Serve hot.

Every inspired scripture has its use for teaching the truth and refuting error, or for reformation of manners and discipline in right living, so that the man who belongs to God may be efficient and equipped for good work of every kind (2 Timothy 3:16-17, NEB).

Famous hostesses have set a style for supper planned around a beautiful tureen of soup. Here's the chance to show off the heirloom soup container from grandmother with extra special food.

ALICIA'S APPLE PUDDING
6 to 8 servings

1 cup granulated sugar
1 cup sifted flour
1 teaspoon baking powder
½ cup (1 stick) butter

6 medium size cooking apples, peeled and cored
1 cup cold water
plain or whipped cream

Preheat oven to 275 degrees. Lightly butter an 8 x 8-inch pan. • Sift together, sugar, flour, and baking powder. Cut butter into dry ingredients with pastry blender or 2 knives until mixture resembles corn meal. Slice apples into prepared pan. Sprinkle flour mixture over apples. Pour 1 cup water carefully over all. • Bake in a very slow oven 50 to 60 minutes. Serve warm with plain or whipped cream.

In those days a decree was issued by the Emperor Augustus for a general registration throughout the Roman world. This was the first registration of its kind; it took place when Quirinius was governor of Syria. For this purpose everyone made his way to his own town; and so Joseph went up to Judaea from the town of Nazareth in Galilee, to be registered at the city of David, called Bethlehem, because he was of the house of David by descent; and with him went Mary who was betrothed to him. She was pregnant, and while they were there the time came for her child to be born, and she gave birth to a son, her first-born. She wrapped him round, and laid him in a manger, because there was no room for them to lodge in the house.

Now in this same district there were shepherds out in the fields, keeping watch through the night over their flock, when suddenly there stood before them an angel of the Lord, and the splendour of the Lord shone round them. They were terror-struck, but the angel said, 'Do not be afraid; I have good news for you: there is great joy coming to the whole people. Today in the city of David a deliverer has been born to you—the Messiah, the Lord. And this is your sign: you will find a baby lying all wrapped up, in a manger.' All at once there was with the angel a great company of the heavenly host, singing the praises of God:

Glory to God in highest heaven,
And on earth his peace for men on whom his favour rests.

After the angels had left them and gone into heaven the shepherds said to one another, 'Come, we must go straight to Bethlehem and see this thing that has happened, which the Lord has made known to us.' So they went with all speed and found their way to Mary and Joseph; and the baby was lying in the manger. When they saw him, they recounted what they had been told about this child; and all who heard were astonished at what the shepherds said. But Mary treasured up all these things and pondered over them. Meanwhile the shepherds returned glorifying and praising God for what they had heard and seen; it had all happened as they had been told (Luke 2:1–20, NEB).

CHRISTMAS

Jesus was born at Bethlehem in Judaea during the reign of Herod. After his birth astrologers from the east arrived in Jerusalem, asking, "Where is the child who is born to be king of the Jews?" (Matthew 2:1–2, NEB).

These recipes may add variety to your traditional family treats. Since Christmas is the Christ Child's birthday, why not celebrate this year with a cake? Happy Birthday, Jesus—one candle to symbolize He is the Light of the World.

Turkey

*Fluffy Quick Brown Rice Stuffing

*Sweet Potato and Apple Casserole

*Black Cherry Salad

Relishes   Coffee

Herb Bread

Birthday Fruitcake

Assorted cookies including

*Pfeffernüsse and *Iris's Ebelskivers

At Christmas it is especially important to plan a dinner which will leave you time to enjoy the day's festivities. The merry Yuletide feast is a happy event honoring Christ's birthday, one to be shared with family and friends. Prepare as much as possible of the menu beforehand. Have the salad and the stuffing for the bird ready in the refrigerator. Bake bread or rolls and prepare desserts ahead and freeze so that they can simply be thawed and reheated.

121

FLUFFY QUICK BROWN RICE STUFFING   *6 cups*

½ pound pork sausage
melted butter or margarine
  (see below)
½ cup onions, chopped
½ cup celery, thinly sliced

1 4-ounce can mushrooms,
  including liquid
2 cups quick-cooking brown
  rice
1 teaspoon salt
3 cups *boiling* water

Break up sausage with fork into small pieces; sauté until golden brown. • Measure fat from sausage and add enough butter or margarine to make ½ cup. (If desired, use ½ cup melted butter or margarine in place of meat fat.) Combine fat, onions, celery, mushrooms, rice, and salt in saucepan. Pour in 3 cups boiling water. Bring to a boil, lower heat, cover tightly, and cook 15 minutes. • This recipe makes 6 cups stuffing. Allow about 1 cup of rice stuffing per pound of ready-to-cook fowl. For 10 to 12-pound turkey, double the above recipe. • Be sure to cool dressing completely before stuffing the bird.

SWEET POTATO AND APPLE CASSEROLE
12 generous servings

3 pounds sweet potatoes
1 pound apples
½ to 1 cup brown sugar,
  packed
¼ cup white sugar

½ teaspoon salt
3 tablespoons butter
¾ cup water
1 teaspoon vanilla extract

The apple in this casserole gives it a distinctive flavor, refreshingly tangy and different from the standard sweet potatoes.

Cook sweet potatoes in skins; peel and slice. Pare and slice apples. Then place alternate layers of sweet potatoes and apples

122

in baking pan. Combine brown sugar, white sugar, salt, butter, water, and vanilla together and boil to make a syrup. Pour the syrup over the potatoes and apples. Bake in 350 degree oven for 45 minutes.

BLACK CHERRY SALAD *10 servings*

2 no. 2½ cans pitted black
  cherries
1 cup crushed pineapple

½ cup grated carrots
1 6-ounce box raspberry gelatin
1 cup walnuts, chopped

Add juice from cherries and pineapple with enough water to make 4 cups. Heat to boiling. Remove from heat, add gelatin, and stir until dissolved. Cool until slightly thickened; stir in carrots. Put some cherries, pineapple, and walnuts in each of 10 molds; fill with gelatin and chill until firm. Unmold and serve on endive; top with mayonnaise.

PFEFFERNÜSSE   *6 dozen cookies*

3 cups sugar
4 cups light corn syrup
¾ cup shortening
1 cup milk
1 teaspoon soda
1 teaspoon allspice

1 teaspoon nutmeg
1 teaspoon cinnamon
¾ teaspoon pepper
grated peel of 4 oranges
flour

Preheat oven to 350 degrees. Lightly grease cookie sheets. • Heat sugar, corn syrup, and shortening together; let cool. Then add milk, soda, allspice, nutmeg, cinnamon, pepper, and grated peel of oranges. Mix in enough flour to make a very stiff dough—it should not stick to hands while kneading. • Take a small amount of dough and make a thin roll, ½ inch in diameter, and cut in small pieces about ¾ inches long with knife or scissors. Continue process until all dough is used. • Put on cookie sheets and bake until light brown. Store in tightly sealed container.

Behold, a virgin shall be with child, and shall bring forth a son, and they shall call his name Emmanuel, which being interpreted is, God with us. Then Joseph being raised from sleep did as the angel of the Lord had bidden him, and took unto him his wife: And knew her not till she had brought forth her firstborn son: and he called his name Jesus (Matthew 1:23–25).

Pretty ice cream balls, hard frozen and ready to be served with eggnog sauce, are an excellent accompaniment to birthday cake or cookies.

The ebelskiver recipe is an old Scandinavian one. Serve ebelskivers warm with lingonberry sauce or confectioners' sugar.

IRIS'S EBELSKIVERS   *24 Ebelskivers*

2 cups all-purpose flour
2 tablespoons sugar
pinch of salt
3 eggs, separated

2 cups buttermilk
1 teaspoon soda, mixed in
   a little hot water

Sift flour, sugar, and salt together. In large mixing bowl, beat egg yolks. Stir soda mixture into buttermilk. Combine the dry ingredients and buttermilk mixture with the egg yolks and mix well. Beat egg whites until stiff; fold into mixture gently. • Cook in well-buttered ebelskiver pan on top of stove, turning once.

124

SWEETHEART BANQUET

Dear friends, let us love one another, because love is from God. Everyone who loves is a child of God and knows God, but the unloving know nothing of God. For God is love; and his love was disclosed to us in this, that he sent his only Son into the world to bring us life (1 John 4:7–10, NEB).

Traditionally, Valentine's Day brings out the romantic heart of the church member. Flowers are the order of the day complete with a meal and musical entertainment featuring such old favorites as "Thine Alone," "Because," and "Always." But because Christ is the center of love, our thoughts turn to 1 Corinthians 13 and 1 John 4:7–12. How better to celebrate the love this day depicts than by fellowshiping together with our Christian brethren?

Mock Pink Champagne
Chicken Cacciatore
Charlotte's Green Peas Continental
Pickled Beets
Coffee   Tea   Rolls   Mints
*Strawberry Pie   *Fudge Pie

Mock pink champagne can be served in champagne glasses, or in sherbets, without offending anyone. By this simple transformation, an otherwise plain punch imparts a festive glamor to this special occasion.

MOCK PINK CHAMPAGNE
8 to 10 servings

½ cup granulated sugar
1 cup water
1 6-ounce can frozen orange
  juice

1 6-ounce can frozen
  grapefruit juice
1 28-ounce bottle chilled ginger
  ale
⅓ cup bottled grenadine syrup

Early in day, mix sugar with water in saucepan and boil 5 minutes. Cool. • Add frozen juice concentrates. Refrigerate. • At serving time add ginger ale and grenadine syrup. Stir lightly. Serve at once in champagne glasses. Makes about 1½ quarts.

CHICKEN CACCIATORE *8 servings*

3 tablespoons flour
1 teaspoon salt
¼ teaspoon black pepper
8 chicken breasts
¼ cup olive oil
1 medium onion, minced
½ cup celery, chopped
½ cup green pepper, chopped

2 tablespoons parsley, chopped
¼ teaspoon garlic powder
1 cup tomato sauce
1 cup canned tomatoes
½ teaspoon sugar
¼ teaspoon orégano
1 cup canned pitted ripe olives

Combine flour, salt, and pepper. Coat chicken with seasoned flour. Heat oil; brown chicken on all sides. • Add all remaining ingredients except ripe olives. • Bring to boil; lower heat. Cover and simmer 25 minutes; add ripe olives. • Cook 15 minutes longer or until chicken is tender when pierced with a fork.

CHARLOTTE'S GREEN PEAS CONTINENTAL
4 servings

2 tablespoons butter
1 clove garlic, halved on
    a toothpick
1 teaspoon prepared mustard

1 teaspoon salt
¼ cup water
1 10-ounce package frozen
    peas
¼ cup pine nuts or almonds

Melt butter with clove of garlic in medium saucepan. Add mustard, salt, water, and frozen peas. Cook until tender. Remove garlic. Place peas in serving dish and sprinkle nuts down the middle.

I may speak in tongues of men or of angels, but if I am without love, I am a sounding gong or a clanging cymbal. I may have the gift of prophecy, and know every hidden truth; I may have faith strong enough to move mountains; but if I have no love, I am nothing. I may dole out all I possess, or even give my body to be burnt, but if I have no love, I am none the better.

Love is patient; love is kind and envies no one. Love is never boastful, nor conceited, nor rude; never selfish, not quick to take offence. Love keeps no score of wrongs; does not gloat over other men's sins, but delights in the truth. There is nothing love cannot face; there is no limit to its faith, its hope, and its endurance.

Love will never come to an end. Are there prophets? their work will be over. Are there tongues of ecstasy? they will cease. Is there knowledge? it will vanish away; for our knowledge and our prophecy alike are partial, and the partial vanishes when wholeness comes. When I was a child, my speech, my outlook, and my thoughts were all childish. When I grew up, I had finished with childish things. Now we see only puzzling reflections in a mirror, but then we shall see face to face. My knowledge now is partial; then it will be whole, like God's knowledge of me. In a word, there are three things that last for ever: faith, hope and love; but the greatest of them all is love (1 Corinthians 13, NEB).

STRAWBERRY PIE   *8 servings*

3 large eggs, separated	3 tablespoons strawberry juice
6 tablespoons granulated sugar	4 tablespoons strawberry
¼ teaspoon salt	gelatin
2 teaspoons lemon juice	¼ teaspoon cream of tartar
1 cup plus 2 tablespoons	6 tablespoons granulated sugar
crushed, fresh or frozen,	½ cup cream, whipped
strawberries	baked 9-inch pie shell or
	vanilla wafer crumb crust

Combine in saucepan the egg yolks and sugar. Then add salt, lemon juice, crushed fresh or frozen strawberries, drained. Cook over low heat, stirring until mixture boils. • Remove from heat;

add strawberry juice and strawberry gelatin to the above mixture and cool. • Beat egg whites until light and frothy. Add the cream of tartar and continue beating until the whites are stiff enough to hold a peak. Gradually beat in the sugar and beat until the meringue is stiff and glossy. Fold in whipped cream. • When the gelatin mixture is practically set, fold in the meringue mixture. • Pile into previously baked 9-inch regular or vanilla wafer crumb shell. Chill 3 hours or more.

Husbands, love your wives, even as Christ also loved the church, and gave himself for it (Ephesians 5:25).

FUDGE PIE   *6 to 8 servings*

⅓ cup butter or margarine
3 1-ounce squares
   unsweetened chocolate
4 eggs, well beaten
2 cups sugar

¼ teaspoon salt
1 teaspoon vanilla extract
⅔ cup pecans, coarsely
   chopped
9-inch unbaked pastry shell
whipping cream, optional

Melt butter or margarine and chocolate in top of double boiler. Cool. • Add eggs and beat well. Then add sugar, salt, and vanilla and beat until thoroughly blended. Add nuts. • Pour into pastry shell and bake in a 350 degree oven for 40 minutes. • Serve cold. Top with whipped cream if desired.

EASTER

. . . they recognized him when he broke the loaf (Luke 24: 35, Phillips).

"Our faith, which overcometh the world," depends on our belief in the resurrection of the crucified Christ. Easter is the day for rejoicing and praise—a day for confirming our belief in the risen Lord.

*Roast Boned Leg of Lamb

Mint Jelly

*Miss Lucy's Tomatoes

Buttered String Beans

*Marian Bruner's Salad

Hot Rolls   Butter

*Aunt Dorothy's Custard Cake or

Lamb Cake

Coffee   Tea

For the lamb cake, use the recipe that comes with the mold. Frost with fluffy icing and sprinkle with coconut. Use a cherry for the nose, raisins for eyes, and place a bow around the neck.

An easier lamb that the children will enjoy is one made of popcorn. Use 1 stick margarine and 6 cups miniature marshmallows, melted in top of double boiler. Add 12 cups seasoned, popped corn. Press into greased mold, allowing an inch of space between halves of mold. Let stand 2 hours. Remove mold, and a nice chubby lamb is ready for any further decoration you desire.

Well-planned party preparations offer a double reward for the hostess—guests *and* hostess at ease to enjoy her hospitality

ROAST BONED LEG OF LAMB
10 servings

Lamb has a particular affinity for sauces. It is also compatible with a wide range of interesting foods and seasonings which make especially attractive and varied dishes. Among the best of them are delicious stews, casseroles, roasts, and skewered shish kebabs.

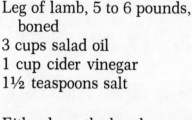

Leg of lamb, 5 to 6 pounds, boned	1 tablespoon sugar
3 cups salad oil	½ teaspoon freshly ground black pepper
1 cup cider vinegar	1 teaspoon thyme
1½ teaspoons salt	1 clove garlic, crushed

Either have the butcher remove the bone from the leg of lamb, or bone it yourself. Also remove the fell or papery outer covering of the roast. Lay lamb flat in glass, earthenware, or any non-metal container. • Combine and mix well the remaining ingredients. Pour over lamb and let stand for 4 hours in the refrigerator. • Remove lamb from marinade and tie into a roll. Roast uncovered for 1½ to 2 hours at 400 degrees.

And while they were still talking about these things, Jesus himself stood among them and said,

"Peace be to you all."

But they shrank back in terror, for they thought they were seeing a ghost.

"Why are you so worried?" said Jesus, "and why do doubts arise in your minds? Look at my hands and my feet—it is really I myself! Feel me and see; ghosts have no flesh or bones as you can see that I have."

But while they still could not believe it through sheer joy, and were quite bewildered, Jesus said to them,

"Have you anything here to eat?"

They gave him a piece of broiled fish and part of a honeycomb, which he took and ate before their eyes (Luke 24: 36–42, Phillips).

MISS LUCY'S TOMATOES   *8 servings*

¼ cup salad oil
2 tablespoons butter,
   melted
4 onions, chopped

2 green peppers, chopped
10 large fresh tomatoes
½ teaspoon sugar
salt and pepper to taste

In oil combined with melted butter, cook onions until golden but not brown. Peel tomatoes and chop; add to onion. Stir. Add green peppers and sugar. • Simmer until reduced by half. Season with salt and pepper to taste. Serve hot.

MARIAN BRUNER'S SALAD   *8 servings*

1 3-ounce package lime
   gelatin
½ cup hot water
1½ cups miniature
   marshmallows
2 8-ounce cans crushed
   pineapple, drained

1 cup pineapple juice
1 cup small curd cottage
   cheese
½ cup whipping cream
1 cup nuts, chopped

In the spring I buy potted geraniums to use in a basket for a centerpiece; later, I put them out in the garden. This way I get double duty from the flowers, rather than having only a few days' enjoyment from cut flowers that will wilt and have to be discarded.

Dissolve gelatin in ½ cup hot water. Add marshmallows and pineapple juice. Heat very slowly until marshmallows are melted. • Let cool until slightly set. Beat until fluffy. Whip whipping cream until stiff. Blend pineapple, cottage cheese, whipping cream, and nuts into jello mixture. • Chill until set.

AUNT DOROTHY'S CUSTARD CAKE
12 to 16 servings

CAKE:

8 egg whites
pinch of salt
⅓ teaspoon cream of tartar
4 egg yolks

1¼ cups granulated sugar
1 cup cake flour
1 teaspoon vanilla extract

Preheat oven to 300 degrees. Beat egg whites until frothy. Add pinch of salt and cream of tartar and beat until stiff and glossy. • In separate bowl beat egg yolks, adding the sugar, flour, and vanilla. Fold into stiffly beaten egg whites. Pour into tube pan and bake for 55 to 60 minutes. • Leave in oven overnight. Invert and remove from tube pan.

SAUCE:

4 egg yolks, beaten
¾ cup granulated sugar
1½ cups sweet milk
2 tablespoons flour
pinch of salt

1 tablespoon unflavored
    gelatin
¼ cup cold water
1 pint whipping cream

Combine eggs, sugar, milk, flour, and salt. Cook until thick. Soften gelatin in ¼ cup cold water; then add to cooked mixture and stir. Cool. Pour over cake. Garnish with 1 pint whipping cream, whipped.

MISSIONARY CONFERENCE WEEK

Instead of the usual baked ham, sliced turkey, or creamed chicken, wouldn't it be more interesting if the food committee (that Committee of Seven) could serve authentic meals from foreign countries? Entrée recipes can be obtained by writing to the respective embassies (a partial list of addresses is included below; all are located in Washington, D.C.). You can also request a flag from the embassies. (It will look great placed appropriately on a wall of your meeting room!) Many embassies will be happy to send you movies depicting geography, native dress, and products of the country.

These additional elements will give a festive flair to the occasion of a missionary's visit. Perhaps you could ask him to give some firsthand impressions of the culture as well as a report about his evangelistic work. A little extra effort and some advance planning will insure your group of an opportunity to get a real "taste" of life in other parts of the world.

Guests welcome pretty settings. Coordinate your tablecloths or mats and napkins with the dominant color scheme provided by the flag of the country you are studying.

AFGHANISTAN
2341 Wyoming Ave., N.W., 20008

ARGENTINA
1600 New Hampshire Ave., N.W., 20009

AUSTRALIA
1601 Massachusetts Ave., N.W., 20036

BRAZIL
3006 Massachusetts Ave., N.W., 20008

BURMA
2300 S St., N.W., 20008

CANADA
1746 Massachusetts Ave., N.W., 20036

CENTRAL AFRICAN REPUBLIC
1618 22d St., N.W., 20008

CHINA
2311 Massachusetts Ave., N.W., 20008

CZECHOSLOVAKIA
3900 Linnean Ave., N.W., 20008

DENMARK
3200 Whitehaven St., N.W., 20008

ETHIOPIA
2134 Kalorama Rd., N.W., 20008

FRANCE
2535 Belmont Rd., N. W., 20008

GERMANY
4645 Reservoir Rd., N.W., 20007

GREAT BRITAIN
3100 Massachusetts Ave., N.W., 20008

GREECE
2221 Massachusetts Ave., N.W., 20008

GUINEA
2112 Leroy Pl., N.W., 20008

HUNGARY
2437 15th St., N.W., 20009

ICELAND
2022 Connecticut Ave., N.W., 20008

INDIA
2107 Massachusetts Ave., N.W., 20008

INDONESIA
2020 Massachusetts Ave., N.W., 20036

IRAN
3005 Massachusetts Ave., N.W., 20008

IRELAND
2234 Massachusetts Ave., N.W., 20008

ISRAEL
1621 22d St., N.W., 20008

ITALY
1601 Fuller St., N.W., 20009

JAPAN
2520 Massachusetts Ave., N.W., 20008

KENYA
2249 R St., N.W., 20008

KOREA
2320 Massachusetts Ave., N.W., 20008

LAOS
2222 S St., N.W., 20008

LIBERIA
5201 16th St., N.W., 20011

MALAYSIA
2401 Massachusetts Ave., N.W., 20008

MEXICO
2829 16th St., N.W., 20009

NEW ZEALAND
19 Observatory Cir., N.W., 20008

NIGERIA
1333 16th St., N.W., 20036

PAKISTAN
2315 Massachusetts Ave., N.W., 20008

PERU
1320 16th St., N.W., 20036

POLAND
2640 16th St., N.W., 20009

SOUTH AFRICA
3051 Massachusetts Ave., N.W., 20008

SPAIN
2700 15th St., N.W., 20009

SWEDEN
600 New Hampshire Ave., N.W., 20037

THAILAND
2300 Kalorama Rd., N. W., 20008

TURKEY
1606 23d St., N.W., 20008

VENEZUELA
2445 Massachusetts Ave., N.W., 20008

VIETNAM
2251 R St., N.W., 20008

Farewell;
I wish you all joy in the Lord.
I will say it again:
all joy be yours.
Philippians 4:4, NEB

ACKNOWLEDGMENTS

To my family for their encouragement and discerning taste for food; to my prayer group for their prayers that I would make it through to the end; to Floyd Thatcher, vice-president and executive editor of Word, Incorporated, who thought the book was a good idea; to my editor, Marjory Leavell, whose eagle eye caught the corrections needed in the recipes; to everyone who shared a recipe; to Marilyn and Gene Scapanski, Wes Michaelson, Jean Schlegel, and Carolyn Banker who knew where the Bible verses were located; to Elizabeth Hatfield, Lucy Lorenzini, Ena Slater, and Mary Rankin who tested some recipes; and to Janet Anderson who typed the manuscript. Thank you.

INDEX